PEERLESS PATRIOTS

Organized Veterans and the Spirit of Americanism

By RODNEY G. MINOTT

Assistant Professor of History,
Stanford University

PUBLIC AFFAIRS PRESS, WASHINGTON, D. C.

440422

To P. K. M. WITH DEVOTION

Copyright, 1962, by Public Affairs Press
419 New Jersey Avenue, S.E., Washington 3, D. C.

Printed in the United States of America
Library of Congress Catalog Card No. 62-22220

FOREWORD

Dr. Rodney G. Minott has written a very significant book dealing with a little understood subject. American self-consciousness, in one form or another, has existed from the 17th century. American national self-consciousness, however, has a shorter history. There are grounds for arguing that the United States came into being prior to the emergence of a strong nationalistic sentiment within the new republic, thus reversing the usual process with which we, living in the 20th century, have grown accustomed. In our own time we have seen scores of peoples, inspired by nationalistic aspirations shake off colonial bonds and erect independent governments sustained by little else save the spirit of nationalism.

At the end of the 19th and opening of the 20th century, groups of Americans sensed a falling off of allegiance to ideals and loyalties characteristic of the predominately rural-oriented, agrarian-commercial culture of 18th and 19th century America in the face of the sweep of industrialism and urbanism, and the influx of millions of immigrants from eastern, southern, and southeastern Europe. The old-timers feared that the new-comers needed a more thorough indoctrination into the traditions and ideals of the republic than chance might afford. Americanization programs appeared having as one of their principal aims the integration of the new into the old. The public schools assumed part of this burden of Americanization, but other groups, including veterans organizations, took upon themselves some of the burden.

It is to the story of the veterans organizations and to their efforts to define that elusive spirit called Americanism and to inform it with a dynamic vitality that Dr. Minott addresses himself. He has also given considerable attention to the work of various veterans organizations in publicizing their views of what constitutes Americanism through committees, programs, and projects. Finally, he has sought to deal with some of the larger problems involving the role of such agencies within the expanded framework of American society and their efforts to help the nation define the goals of the common life.

GEORGE HARMON KNOLES

iii

PREFACE

Like any historian making acknowledgments, I feel staggered by the task of trying to pay tribute to all the authors, past and present, who have contributed to my endeavors. A check of my sources, of course, gives a fairly precise indication of who they are. I have drawn upon many of them for the stimulation of ideas and cited others in support of conclusions. Sadly, perhaps too many persons who are not listed aided me in various ways without my being fully aware of their contributions. I hope that this meager salute will suffice in their case for obviously no one has a monopoly on ideas and interpretation.

Specifically, I would like to thank a number of persons here at Stanford University and elsewhere for helping me, but all the while emphasizing that any errors of fact or faulty judgment remain solely my responsibility. Professors Thomas A. Bailey of Stanford and Frank Freidel of Harvard early gave me encouragement when this study was in its infancy. Special thanks must go to Professor David M. Potter of Stanford, who aided me by bringing his remarkable insight and imagination to bear upon the whole confusing problem of nationalism. I am beholden to a host of immediate colleagues and friends for help in reading and furnishing valuable criticism of my manuscript. Among them are: Professor Otis Pease and Charles McLaughlin of Stanford's history department, Professor David Levin of Stanford's English department, Professors Jon M. Bridgman of the University of Washington's history department and Richard Cramer of the department of history, San Jose State College. Evelyn Stewart at the University of California (Berkeley) furnished many invaluable ideas. Finally, I am forever indebted to Mrs. Peter Kmetovic of Palo Alto, California, for her patience and skill in editing, deciphering and retyping copy that resembled ancient Chinese manuscripts. Only a Higher Being could reward her properly.

RODNEY G. MINOTT

Stanford University

ABOUT THE AUTHOR

Rodney G. Minott was born in Portland, Oregon, and received his secondary education in Concord, Massachusetts. Upon graduating from preparatory school he found the lure of military adventure too strong to resist. Just as World War II ended he abandoned college plans and enlisted in the Regular Army of the United States, serving overseas in the Pacific. Put on inactive duty he entered Stanford University but returned to active military life during the Korean Conflict.

Upon discharge from the Army, he re-entered Stanford. In 1960 he received his Ph.D. as an Americanist specializing in social and intellectual history. He now teaches at Stanford as an Assistant Professor where he has also been the Assistant Director of the Western Civilization Program. *Peerless Patriots* is his first book. Currently he has in preparation *The Image of the Soldier in American Fiction,* and *Alpenfestung! The Myth of the Nazi Redoubt.*

CONTENTS

CHAPTER I

INTRODUCTION

It used to be said that brave men die but once and cowards many times. In wars fought for the nation-state, where all are bidden to sacrifice for God and country, cowards often do not have to die at all, but the eternal sensibilities of the brave cause them mortification a thousandfold.

History witnesses that with nationalistic idealism Americans walked up Cuba's San Juan Hill in 1898 only to vitiate such spirit by 1901 a world apart in the savage suppression of the Philippine's independence. As a people armed with righteousness, we marched on a patriotic crusade to make the world safe for democracy in 1917, and then asked ourselves later in wonderment or cynicism about the price of such glory. Grimly national in our martial unity and with justifiable moral cause in World War II, we struck down the perversion of genocide, but in the end our consciences uneasily noted that it was not just the enemy who was capable of exterminating whole peoples. And, to a large extent, that problem has remained. Due to circumstances that we certainly have not created entirely by ourselves, the dubious questions involved in nuclear defense have not solved the dilemma of how to maintain national self-interest while steering clear of extinction. In each of the foregoing episodes it seems to have been the belief that American ideals, traditions, and rights were threatened if we did not fight, yet in each case material and ethical problems were produced which cast doubt upon our ultimate war aims.

What is the "national self-interest"? These days does patriotism include the proposition that we who love America are free to aid in obliterating the peoples of the world in defense of our ideals? Are such actions a defensible policy now? And, indeed, what forces within history have conspired to produce a national will which must attempt to solve on a collective basis questions of life and death that, in classic understatement, are highly personal?

An explanation of what nationalism is and how it has operated is a subject that requires some background, for this magnetic mystique has proven to be one of the most pervasive influences in twentieth century society. In truth, no age and few peoples have ever escaped a form of self-infatuation. The ancient Hebrews knew themselves to be God's chosen few, and the cultural snobbery of the Greeks in the classical age has been so durable that it remains an important factor in the history of Western Civilization. But the form that nationalism has taken in the last century and a half must be of special concern to our generation. Whereas nationalism has often worked to preserve races and societies in the past, recently it has done the reverse and it now obviously stands to destroy three thousand years of man's efforts in building civilization.

Americans, like most people in the world today, are painfully aware that they can be shattered in an instant should their leaders or leaders elsewhere miscalculate. Our citizens are not as sure of the role nationalism and its supporters have played and will play in this drama of potential death. Truthfully, thousands of persons motivated by the sincerest beliefs to protect and preserve what they assume to be the national heritage stagger down history's highway bewildered and ignorant of when, how, and why patriotism has worked either for their interests or against them.

Among the most dedicated and ardent American nationalists attempting to cope with the nebulous ideals of patriotism are those men and women enrolled in organized veterans' societies. All our wars have produced ex-servicemen's groups and several excellent books already have been written concerning those founded during the nineteenth century. Other equally informative books have been written about only two of the major veterans' organizations founded in this century, the rest, for some reason, being ignored. This chronicle deals with eight chosen because of the wars they represent, their social composition, and their impact upon the nation. Furthermore, the emphasis is upon those special committees within the larger bodies that are concerned with nationalism, sovereignty, patriotic ritual, and how they attempt to adapt such abstractions to the exigencies of our turbulent age. The organizations are: The United Spanish War Veterans, the Veterans of the Foreign Wars of the United States, the American Legion, the Military Order of the World Wars, the Disabled American Veterans, the Military Order of the Purple Heart, the American Veterans Committee, and the American Veterans of World War II and Korea.[1]

There is a tendency for men who are ignorant of the past to be fearful and resentful of the present because they do not understand what transpired before to produce their immediate circumstances. In their anger and frustration such persons often seek refuge in the fortress of a romanticized vision of history as they wish it to have been. They create their own realities, and historical facts that rupture the image are ignored or censored so that the dream will persist and protect them. Large numbers of the veteran class have fallen heir to practicing such self-delusion. Perhaps this is because many have made very extensive sacrifices for the nation in this century, but they have experienced a bafflement when reentering civil life to find that society takes their war services for granted and that time has changed the land and home they left. Many ex-soldiers have rationalized their unease over new events by believing that their military service must indicate and represent something special to give them status under such perplexing conditions. Part of such status symbolism has been an attempt to link duty on the nation's behalf with the country's history, the only trouble being that the average veteran has an imprecise grasp on the facts of his nation's traditions. Quite frequently he has chosen to emphasize only those aspects in our heritage that enhance his preconceived stereotypes, primarily because they are comforting and boost his self-esteem.

The veteran is not, of course, the only person at fault for doing this. His critics, sometimes as ignorant of history as he is, lambast organized ex-servicemen too often without due appreciation for those currents, events, and presures of history that have helped to make the veteran, his ideals, and his actions what they are. Both talk and write extensively about the true meaning of national glory and the virtues of the American character. Much in the history of the United States is unique but not as unique as many of us believe. There is no point in trying to tell the twentieth-century veterans' story and ascertain the motives behind their patriotic programs without giving a very generalized historical account of the rise of modern nationalism. These programs did not just happen; they have to be seen in the glow of historical events. Our basic institutions, such as language, law, and political theory, were largely given to us by the British. As for American nationalism and our sense of patriotism, it belongs to a mosaic depicting the evolution of modern nationalism emanating from the French Revolution of 1789 and as it has affected all the nations in Western society since then. Ours is but one story among many, and the tale reflects courage and cowardice, cynicism and idealism in regard to national glory and the virtues of that most obscure concept referred to as the American character. As a people, have we always maintained the noblest aspirations and been models of rectitude and if we have, will these qualities forever endure? The answer to the first question is "hardly" and the second one remains unanswerable.

Valiant as the conduct of our Revolutionary War soldiers was, it is well to remember that the Americans of that era were bitterly divided on the question of the revolution. Furthermore, enlistments in the regular or Continental Army were a continual problem to Washington. A hard, tiny core of men dedicated to the principles of the Declaration of Independence won that fight, but they could not have done so without French aid and the fact that Britain was engaged in a world war and not simply fighting Americans. Much of the suffering borne by Washington's troops occurred because of the indifference, selfishness and hostility of their fellow Americans. Nor for a generation after the war for independence were all Americans unified in their love and appreciation of the national state. During the War of 1812 sectionalism almost gutted the war effort against Great Britain as the 1814 Hartford Convention saw some New Englanders threaten to secede from the union over President James Madison's war policies. A paradox followed the War of 1812, for as Americans finally appeared unified and were swept up in the nationalistic expansion to the west which they called Manifest Destiny, a sectional nationalism presaged the eventual Civil War of the sixties.[2]

The sad rupture between the North and the South and our subsequent patriotism cannot be understood without an extremely simplified recalling of certain historical trends afoot in both Europe and the United States between the period of the French Revolution of 1789 and the Spanish-America War of 1898. One of the most devasting by-products of the French Revolution was the phenomenon of modern nationalism. In France the absolutism of their kings was replaced by the absolutism of the people, expressed through what the philosopher Jean Jacques Rousseau called the common will. The revolutionary leaders urged the citizens to fuse their hearts and minds emotionally and intellectually with the ideal of the nation-state. Formerly, men had been used to pledging their loyalty to institutions such as a royal dynasty, a religion, or a political body. In the world's history since that era men have given their love to an emblematical ideal of the state and society in unity. In fact, the love has been offered so unrestrainedly and with such zeal it amounts to a type of religion. One form of this deification and identification with the nation-state is termed patriotism.

The armies of France carried the spirit of the new nationalism across all of Europe, first under revolutionary leadership and later under Napoleon in the early nineteenth century. In many areas of Europe, however, there was an intense reaction against the French conquests and, borrowing from their temporary masters, the peoples of Spain, Germany, and the central and eastern European countries revolted, and in the process created their own unique nationalism based upon local cultures. Intellectuals were in the forefront of the Napoleonic revolts and nowhere were they more articulate than in Germany where they not only rebelled against the French, but conditioned by the philosophy of Romantic Idealism, they reacted against the rational abstractions of the eighteenth-century Enlightenment. Such German nationalists as Johann Gottlieb Fichte and Friedrich Ludwig Jahn, instead of emphasizing the Enlightenment tenets of mankind's similarity and the universal rights that came to him naturally, stressed the historical, cultural, racial, and mystically spiritual differences of the Germans that set them apart from other peoples.[3]

Such beliefs did not stay confined to Germany alone. Between the end of the Napoleonic period and the 1840's, a fusion of French revolutionary principles, German Romantic Idealism and the new nationalism produced a series of revolutionary agitations led by young, fervently patriotic intellectuals who wished to circumscribe the power of their leaders by liberal constitutions. The youth of many nations, including those of Italy, Ireland, and the Latin American countries, engaged in revolutionary movements during the thirties and forties, led by such men as the Italian Guiseppe Mazzini, the Irishman Daniel O'Connell, the Argentinian Jose de San Martin, and the Venezuelan Simon Bolivar. Attendant to political and social revolts were the cultural efforts of the intellectuals who contributed to the nationalistic impulse by writing histories of the community that stressed folk-myths and traditions peculiar only to their peoples. A spate of historical research took place during the period as the scholars diligently and imaginatively set about to discover or create a composite self-image which could be called the national character.

These impelling forces took different forms in each country, so it would be a flagrant oversimplification to say that the same experiences taking place in Europe and South America had an exact duplication in the United States. Very similar events and currents of thought, however, found a close parallel in American letters. Many of our writers and thinkers, like their European counterparts, were strongly conditioned by both nationalism and romanticism. James Fenimore Cooper, William Cullen Bryant, Jared Sparks, Herman

Melville, and Washington Irving, to name but a few, all strove to create a literature whose themes, idioms and protagonists could only be identified as culturally native. The same practices were adopted by those writers who specialized in historical narrative. Best known of the early nineteenth-century American historians who studied in Germany and predicated an idealistic, patriotic thesis of United States history was George Bancroft. He was joined at a later period by Francis Parkman, who, while not trained in Germany, wrote histories of the struggle between France and England for control of North America that strongly reflected a cultural nationalism analogous to that found in Europe. According to Parkman and his colleagues, the northern Protestant, Anglo-Saxon or Teutonic societies displayed a vigor and a resourcefulness that made them the natural superiors of the southern Catholic, Latin peoples as well as the savages of North America. It was these alleged factors of race, religion, and democratic impulses stemming from the tribes of ancient Germany and subsequently passed on to Britain and America that accounted for the Anglo-American victories over the French and their Indian allies. The histories as written by the likes of Bancroft and Parkman in the generation between 1830 and 1860 were masterpieces of literary style. The books were widely read and their postulates taken to heart by the public, but it is well to remember that the inherent racism in those works was of a comparatively innocent variety compared to that of later generations.[4]

Much of this type of history written on both sides of the Atlantic displays a raggedly unscientific attempt to ascertain and explain why certain races appeared to have an organic unity possessing similar characteristics which made them more powerful, materially successful and progressive than others. The trouble with such a superficial analysis was that it eventually smashed into the mystical force of modern state nationalism as it, in turn, became conditioned by industrialism, capitalism, urbanization, and the theories of biological evolution. The result of this devil's brew accounts for much of the perverted nationalism that has corroded the minds of too many Americans and Europeans from the latter part of the nineteenth century until the present.

Nationalism began to change in the middle of the nineteenth century in Europe and America. Up to about 1848 it stressed the cultural uniqueness of a geographic area in hopes that this would establish and enhance a society's superiority. The European nationalistic movements also placed great reliance upon the principles of liberalism with its tenets of the rights of the individual, humanitarian reforms and constitutional limitations on political power. These middle-class surges toward social and political equality culminated in the widespread revolutions of 1848. But the dazzling expectations of the revolutionaries turned to sour disillusionment as many of the rebellions were either squashed or as the leaders in some countries frittered away their chances to enact liberal programs and thus allowed the forces of conservatism to regroup and reassert control once more. The revolutionary period saw a major transformation of nationalism for, henceforth, unity of the society to buttress the power of the state was emphasized over individual rights. As an example, in 1852 Louis Napoleon of France was freely elected but he ruled as a dictator until toppled in 1870. Among the tactics he used to maintain power were the exploitation of his family name and a domestic policy that promised social welfare given by the national state. The German reformers, too, transmuted their liberal aspirations into national ones which by 1871 helped the conservative Prussian Otto von Bismark to create Imperial Germany. That unhappy nation became a hyper-nationalistic society peculiarly composed of a highly efficient industrial economy presided over by a romantically medieval authoritarian power elite. Advanced social welfare benefits were utilized with the purpose of tying the populace to the state and not necessarily given out of humanitarian intentions.[5]

Americans suffered from the complexities of new social and economic forces as did Europeans at the mid-century. Here the agrarian South self-consciously proclaimed its unique cultural differences from the increasingly urbanized, industrialized North. At the heart of the problem lay the question of the slave system serving a one crop economy, and during the fifties Southerners, in defense of their "peculiar institution," began to talk in terms of nationalistic self-determination. The social and cultural differences of the Southern way of life became a large factor in the Southern attempts to justify the existence of chattel servitude. Borrowing heavily from the romantic novels of Sir Walter Scott, many persons south of the Mason-Dixon Line created a synthetic legend of the aristocratic-cavalier tradition of the area which sharply constrasted with the supposed materialistic society of the North. Southern constitutionalists, such as John C. Calhoun and Roger B. Taney, offered arguments stating that slavery was good for the nation since the South's economy depended upon it. Because it was condoned by the Bible and the Negro was naturally inferior to the whites, slavery was the obvious system to keep the two races living in peace. Furthermore, it was pointed out, legally slaves were private property and the Federal Constitution guaranteed property rights. According to Calhoun, the final source of sovereign power lay not with the national government which had had been created by the states, but with the local governments. If the Congress enacted laws which the citizens felt to be unconstitutional, they could declare them so and take appropriate action, up to and including secession. Surely such a doctrine was the quintessence of local, individualistic nationalism.

Northerners, taking their cue from Daniel Webster's famous 1830 speech on the theory of the Union, responded that states' rights indicated treason to the national government. The Constitution may have been created by the people, but this meant the entire populace and it could not be undone by disenchanted special groups. By 1861 the two Constitutional interpretations of American nationalism clashed militarily and the people fought savagely. When the tragedy ended, states' rights nationalism was a spectre but a durable shade, to be sure. However, despite some contemporary Southern insistence that the Federal government is neither morally nor legally empowered to enforce desegregation, the arguments have been more emotional than legally effective. The question of who possesses the power to enforce national sovereignty has been settled since Grant met Lee at Appomattox Court House in the spring of 1865.[6]

As the scholarly expert on nationalism, Professor Hans Kohn of The College of the City of New York, has demonstrated, the Civil War and Reconstruction coincided with the Italian and German wars of national unification from 1859 to 1871. The Northern victory, despite the grave problems produced during Reconstruction, preserved national unity and the traditions of individual liberty were maintained. In much of Europe, by contrast, an opposite pattern developed, as national unity produced strong governments created at the expense of local power, humanitarianism and liberal individualism. Pan-nationalistic movements swept Germany and the Slavic peoples, where the emphasis lay on a racial reunion of ethnically similar peoples beyond the nation's border. Hence, in Germany certain pressure groups demanded a racial brotherhood of the European Aryan peoples which would dominate the racially inferior Slavs and Jews of the continent. In Russia a similar movement grew which wished to incorporate all the Slav-speaking peoples into the Tsar's empire. But, according to Professor Kohn's interpretation, the American experience differed greatly, for the history of liberty and tolerance was so strong that millions of persons who emigrated here following the Civil War were fused into a spiritual and national unity.[7]

The story, while true in many respects, has not been quite that brilliantly successful. The Northern victory and the abolition of slavery did shine magnificently outside the borders of the United States, and millions of people did indeed pour into the nation from across the seas. Yet Americans cannot take that occurrence with conceit and at face value, for both our earlier history and the Civil War left legacies in regard to native racism that plague us yet, just as ethnicism gripped so many Europeans as the nineteenth century closed and the twentieth began. The United States' immediate race problems were its traditional ones—the Negro and the Indian. As the former was freed, he still was denied equality and the latter was either inexorably degenerated or destroyed. Both were reduced to the status of subcultures. Yet, paradoxically the fight against slavery created a whole new series of unforeseen racial problems not related to Negroes and Indians but in regard to the immense immigration that began soon after the Civil War. Inspired in part by the North's victory and the American democratic image, scores came to the United States escaping varieties of persecution in Europe. Their reception in the land of promise was apt to be a miserably humiliating one. The question of why this was so has remained one of the salient problems confronting twentieth-century American society, and this whole social experience has been an integral part of the reshaping of American nationalism and its ritualism of patriotic practice.

In trying to absorb the immigrant and handle questions of race, the twentieth-century patriot has been dealing with several interwoven historical problems in connection with what he regards as the proper national image. How and where does the alien fit into our society was the leading question for thousands of Americans who belonged to patriotic groups and brotherhoods. Cultural and racial assimilation came to occupy a disproportionate amount of the organized veterans' time and energies because the very fact of alien blood symbolized an impurity which affronted numerous native-born citizens. Genetics increasingly became a powerful factor in modern patriotism with great emotional appeal, since it holds attraction for minds that are either irrational or intellectually untrained. The impact of Darwinian evolutionary theory did not help clarify the vision of numerous patriots gathered in fraternal bonds.

Many Americans and Europeans have continued to subscribe to the pseudo-scientific doctrines of Social Darwinism, whereby it has been "proven" that the principles of biological evolution could be applied to human societies with only the "fittest surviving." Actually, Social Darwinism taken alone has not been the only force that eventually produced the modern-day extermination camps. In America, for instance, it more often has been applied to economic and commercial competition; but what it has done in the realm of nationalism has been to lend credibility to those Americans and Europeans who wished to invoke the magic name of science to support racism. Often such theories neatly substantiated the pre-Darwinian contentions that the peoples of North European and Anglo-Saxon stock truly were superior races. In Germany these traditional elements of racialism were tragically underscored by Social Darwinism which aided in clearing the paths leading to such infamous places as Buchenwald.

In America the story of eugenics being adapted to patriotic programs has not had such a wretched outcome, but biological nationalism has been an important quantity in the fashioning of the patriots' so-called national character. Social Darwinism was especially prevalent in the minds of many persons from the period of 1890 to about the time of World War I. For such a reason the era merits a special word in this introductory chapter, for it was during that epoch that a majority of the American veterans' societies of the present fashioned their stereotype of the nation. Having created it, the product has remained with them to the present. The United States, as most of today's organized veterans officially have preferred to view it, is a society whose basic principles have been shaped by what Professor Richard Hofstadter of Columbia University calls "the *mystique* of Anglo-Saxonism." This has not meant an especially pro-British attitude, but rather an oversimplified and racially romantic orientation toward the Nordic Protestant cultures heavily buttressed by Social Darwinian theory. Why such thoughts were so attractive and so readily subscribed to should be easy to see in view of the earlier nineteenth-century historical literature which used such themes as exemplified by Parkman and Bancroft even before the advent of Social Darwinism. Also, before evolutionary doctrines became popularized, Americans were already conditioned by the virulent anti-Catholic, antiforeign sentiment of the 1850's, the slavery issue, territorial expansion against the Mexicans, the degraded condition of the freed Negro following the Civil War, and the continual frontier Indian fighting.[8]

During the 1890's groups of important Americans became entranced with the beliefs that hearkened back to those earlier nineteenth-century historians who wrote expressively about the alleged superiorities of the Anglo-Saxon heritage. Apparently they did not fully realize that others before them had predicated very much the same thesis because their writings, such as those of Connecticut's John Fiske, who lectured at Harvard, reflect an absolute rapture of discovery. Much of their thinking was directed along lines of imperialism, influenced and symbolized by the naval theorist Alfred Thayer Mahan whose book, *The Influence of Seapower upon History, 1660-1783*, appeared in 1890. Numbers of historians, political theorists, ministers, and politicians took up the cry. Theodore Roosevelt not only studied Mahan but listened intently as Professor John W. Burgess of Columbia University Law School lectured to students on the peerless excellence of the Anglo-Saxon political genius and the role the Aryan races had and were playing in ruling lesser breeds. Roosevelt took it all very much to mind and heart, and for the remainder of his life the questions of territorial expansion, race, and the ethnic origins of his fellow Americans were of the deepest interest and concern to him. And he was not the only one in his preoccupation with such as a tradition. As Professor Hofstadter points out in his book, *Social Darwinism in American Thought*, one of the most strident voices of the time enunciating racist Anglo-Saxon theory belonged to the Reverend Josiah Strong whose ". . . uncanny capacity for assimilating the writings of Darwin . . . to the prejudices of rural Protestant America . . . " made Strong not only a symbolic figure of the period but a man of great popularity. He was anti-immigration, anti-Catholic, anti-liquor, and anti-urbanism among many other things. But extremist as Strong was, many of his beliefs were echoed by conservative politicians as well. Republican Senator Albert J. Beveridge exhorted Americans who sprang "from the most masterful blood in history" to rule those incapable of self-government because "Fellow-Americans, we are God's chosen people . . . His great purposes are revealed in the progress of the flag . . . "[9]

These leaders of American politics and molders of opinion were not without contemporary critics. But the influence of men like Roosevelt, Beveridge, and Massachusetts' Republican Senator Henry Cabot Lodge, all of whom shared similar beliefs, was extensive and they were prominent in national affairs from the time of the Spanish-American War to the period of the First World War. It should be noted that it was between 1890 and 1920 that the largest twentieth-century veterans' organizations were founded. Of all those personages the one who seems to have exerted the most enduring effect in certain respects upon the veterans' societies founded in that period was Theodore Roosevelt. It was T. R.'s personal brand of patriotism and it was the America that shaped his character which became the core of patriotic belief for millions of organized veterans. If these ex-servicemen can be said to have had a patriotic ideologist, it was Theodore Roosevelt.

In many ways the veterans could not have selected a better symbol nor a worse one. No one loved his country more and no man was physically braver, a fact he felt compelled to demonstrate repeatedly throughout his life. But his patriotism was exuberantly muscular and unilateral. He practiced the strenuous life which delighted his hard working countrymen, but he could also refer to Latin Americans as "brown monkeys" and brag without fear of reprisal how he personally "seized" Panama. At present we live in an age when millions of Americans bitterly resent the restrictions placed upon them by the realities of our precarious existence and, as outlined earlier, there is the tendency on the part of many persons to retreat from reality by trying to recapture and re-enter an imaginary, controllable society. Many of the veterans collectively have indicated a wish to recreate Roosevelt's America as they have demanded less government control at home but more militancy abroad. The problem is that history may neither be reversed nor escaped.

If the veterans truly understood the spirit of the first Roosevelt, they might note three things upsetting to several current official beliefs about Rooseveltian patriotism: he believed strongly in civil liberties, save for one brief sorry period; he believed in a powerful chief executive who would use the implied constitutional powers of the presidency as readily as would a later Roosevelt; and his martial belligerency was an oddity which was considered both childish and dangerous even by many of his contemporaries. Roosevelt felt that America was becoming a complex society where Congress and the courts of the day represented special interests. Accordingly, strong executive leadership was needed to keep the big business trusts regulated so they would not dominate the government as they did the economy. This political philosophy, however, has not suited much of the contemporary official attitudes of veterans' organizations so they have tended to ignore it. Too, they have fearfully tried to compromise civil rights, sometimes in regard to the fight for racial equality and at other times in the name of preserving the national traditions against radical Marxism. Sadly, the veterans of later years have, as they invoke his name and spirit, discarded in Roosevelt's career all those elements which might compromise the current officially approved patriotic *mystique*.[10]

In their concern with the virtues of the martial spirit, the veterans have often extolled the type exhibited by Roosevelt and his generation of intrepid comrades at San Juan Hill as well as his willingness to talk toughly about international affairs. A man killed at San Juan Hill died just as surely as one killed in later conflicts, but the battle itself was to be succeeded by far more ghastly and serious ones. Furthermore, its intoxicating effect on Roosevelt makes a later generation, which has been raised on a diet of slaughter, wonder about the appropriateness of his military ardor. His boast of how he killed a Spaniard like a rabbit has unfortunate connotations for men today whose future is so hazardous and whose memories include Lidice, Nagasaki, and the 1956 Hungarian Revolt. Indeed, many of Roosevelt's ideas on war were absurd. To him it was a personal experience to prove his manhood to himself and San Juan suited the occasion admirably. He found his meager hours there to have been the apex of his life, but he seems not to have grasped the full implications of land and air warfare that evolved after 1898 and which his sons so bravely endured in the two world wars. As late as 1917 he romantically wished to lead troops of mounted cavalry against the entrenched machine guns of the Kaiser's army. How realistic then have the veterans been in attempting to use the Rooseveltian belligerent spirit peculiar to his own personality and of his ingenuous age to suit events of the more recent past? Physical bravery should not be denigrated *per se;* it has served our nation brilliantly in the past and is doing so now from Berlin to Southeastern Asia. But today the ultimate issue has not been a choice of war and peace, but of annihilation or of entering into an economic and psychological endurance contest. The activist military measures so belovedly summoned forth in the name of national glory by the veterans' leadership may be infectious to a people notoriously impatient for they have worked before in our history, but the historian notes that many times such calls have fallen upon deaf ears despite the ex-servicemen's clarion appeals.[11]

The changing nature of war has not meant that armies and the veteran class have been rendered quite obsolete. Technological changes in fighting equipment, such as use of the horse, gunpowder, breechloading weapons, and nuclear power, have all worked revolutions in military hierarchies, techniques, and the societies that support them. But however important the changes, they traditionally have taken long periods of time to be accomplished. Accordingly, after gunpowder was in use, soldiers still wore parts of armor; massed formations during the Civil War were used in spite of the fact that rapid-fire breechloading rifles and carbines existed; the machine gun has been standard in all armies for a little over half a century, but some horse cavalry was still in use by World War II. Nations and people resist change but, even while adjusting to new conditions, they will continue to make use of customs, institutions, policies, and artifacts of the civilization that has served them in the past even if they are obsolete.

It was thought in the West that nuclear war would abolish armies since, in actuality, no one could win such a conflict in the traditional sense. Even some Communist nations now apparently feel this to be so. If there were no wars as a matter of course, the veterans' class would eventually wither away. This has not happened, however, due to the innate conservative perversity of man—the political animal who now attempts, in a military sense, to have his cake and eat it, too. Both the United States and Russia have evolved a curiously dual war policy which at least takes official note that a nuclear war would solve nothing. The Soviets, however, following the dialectical dogma on Western imperialism, have announced that rebellions against governments friendly to America represent wars of liberation against colonial-capitalist domination. Such wars may be supported by a variety of means with the presumed hope that they will not flare out of control. The United States quite naturally has finally countered the Russian moves by establishing special military programs whereby our troops act as unofficial counterrevolutionaries training the soldiers of our allies on how to meet rebel guerrilla tactics with effective measures of their own. Such wars are being supported in a number of places and by a variety of means, also with the presumed hope that they will not flare out of control. Meanwhile, in both countries large military establishments continue in being while experiments with nuclear rocketry go on and diplomats jockey with and juggle around the problem of some form of disarmament.[12]

Given the dynamics of the East-West struggle, several facts stand out. Americans have clearly demonstrated that they have no intention of giving way before the inexorable thrusts of the Communists. And as long as *any* type of warfare has been thought to be feasible, armies will continue to exist, thus perpetuating an ex-servicemen's class. We have fought four major wars in the last half century, and at the present there are about twenty-two million ex-soldiers who have served in those conflicts. Roughly four million have been organized into societies.[13]

Citizens who love their country, both those within and those without the veterans' groups, often have been at odds over what methods must be used to meet threats to our country. Our leaders call upon us to defend the faith of our fathers but that faith differs from individual to individual. By and large, the veterans have assumed the responsibility of defining what the national image should be and what it has been in the past. In doing so they have consistently attempted to inculcate a form of patriotic spirit among the people of the United States. The veterans' associations and their critics, however, seem to have been undecided about the precise role played by them in fostering nationalism. In the twentieth century much patriotic sentiment has been loosely classified as Americanism, but no one appears sure of the exact meaning of the term. Its imprecision has been a continuing problem that both pleases and bedevils some of the larger veterans' groups.

Despite its abstract nature, Americanism has been a fact of our social existence and will be perpetuated. Its basis is loyalty, but America has a fluid, cosmopolitan society with shifting values and possesses a diversity of loyalties. The *mystique* of national patriotism must compete with a myriad of subattachments. People who have shared common experiences and beliefs often group together and the basis of such a coalition is one form of loyalty. By banding together, men have found not only strength in collectivity but emotional security. Millions of Americans have incorporated themselves for just such purposes and the veterans have done so, too, thereby providing a sense of identity and enhanced self-prestige for each member.[14]

Another possible function of the veterans' groups has been to serve as a link between the national symbols of Americanism and subloyalties. In such an instance, the ambiguities of Americanism have been both a help and a hindrance. Because Americanism is so amorphous, the ex-servicemen have been able, as they wished, to identify self-interest with national interests. Understandably, individuals within these organizations have reacted on the country's behalf with regard to their immediate social groups. Persons outside the corporations, however, have asked how ethical it has been to identify self-interest with the national good. A great many individuals (not necessarily organized veterans) have also expressed entirely personal views in the name of patriotism, but the veterans especially have been singled out for censure. It has been the price they have paid for appointing themselves as national patriotic arbiters.

During the twenties and the depression thirties persons questioned the conduct of veterans' fraternities. With good reason some deplored their apparently commercialized patriotism. The soldiers' official policies often were selfish and cloaked in the flag, but in examining their actions, those who have objected to them have failed to view the veteran problem comprehensively. Critical books and articles have appeared demonstrating that the ex-servicemen have been motivated by economic determinism. Other authors thought that they saw the sinister shadows of native fascism in the various associations' chauvinism. Some of the charges have not been entirely baseless. Often, however, the allegations have been too sweeping and superficial and have long needed reappraisal.

Because the veterans' bloc in society has been a relatively large one in the recent past and since the oppressive nature of the times will maintain them as a class, its former and present influence in the body politic should be examined and analyzed. Of all the struggles we have faced the present one has offered the most challenges to our spiritual and material resources, and only the passage of history will reveal the ultimate outcome. All our contests have seen us enter the fray with one set of national ideals and goals only to have them transmuted before the strife has ended. In regard to such a phenomenon, it might be well to see whether or not the veterans' concepts of Americanism have also changed in this tormented century, since patriotic national self-interest has been the motivating force behind these wars and those who served have played the major roles. A historical look at the organized veterans of the twentieth century and their programs will not answer the impatient question of what these fervent nationalists will do for good or evil in the future. History never solves such problems, but it has demonstrated that given enough time all perplexities are altered or converted into something that they were not originally. The chronicle that follows illustrates such a point, for whatever they wish for the future they cannot escape history.

Chapter II

THE SPANISH WAR VETERANS UNITE

Who remembers, much less cares, about them now? The names of William Rufus Shafter and Nelson Miles evoke nothing to a generation concerned about the immediate actions and personalities of Charles De Gaulle, John F. Kennedy, Mao Tse-tung, and Nikita Khrushchev. Yet once Russell Alger, William T. Sampson, and George Dewey created as much attention as do the names of contemporary bigwigs and astronauts. Only a little over sixty years ago Miles and Shafter commanded the American Army in its expedition against the Spaniards in Cuba. Alger was the Secretary of War presiding over a department that was unprepared to fight, while Sampson and Dewey led naval squadrons which defeated the enemy fleet at Santiago Harbor and Manila Bay. Along with others who fought, Sampson and Dewey were singled out by the press and public as representative heroes and they reigned briefly as such.

Under the frantic pressure of subsequent affairs they have all been forgotten, but, historically, theirs was an important role in the evolution of modern patriotism. They brought the heritage of nineteenth century America with them into the twentieth, which meant to them that the divisiveness of sectionalism must be closed by national unity. They also carried with them the provincialism of their age, and this often took the form of ethnic prejudices. It has been their fate to have desired unity while finding themselves bewildered by having to live the major portion of their existence in an era where the whole society was increasingly mobilized and regimented to meet a host of undreamed of crises. In such an atmosphere the fundamentalist individualism that helped shape their characters has been on the defensive against the twentieth century. In patriotic affairs they have passed onto their successors among the veterans' groups many of the psychological scars incurred in these conflicts and thus the soldiers and sailors of the Spanish-American War are formative as well as transitional figures in the creation of the current veterans' associations. One foot has remained in a prior century while the

other has taken steps into the present. In order to understand
modern patriotism we must first look at those who belong to yester-
year.

*   *   *

The war with Spain in 1898 was both successful and popular. Compared to the wars that followed the Cuban adventure seemed almost
a comic-opera interlude to later generations. Yet recent reappraisals
of the Spanish-American War show that Americans entered it in a
spirit of genuine idealism. Neither sinister machinations by the
business world nor the sensational yellow press instigated the war.
In part, the war resulted from American expansionist sentiments, but
even many reformers, those who had been agrarian Populists and
those who became urban Progressives, favored war. The nation embarked on a moral crusade to exorcise the evil of Old World tyranny
symbolized by decadent, Catholic Spain.[1]

The war brought a state of euphoria to prosperous, nationalistic
America. The antagonism between the urban and rural elements
of society dimmed and the wounds of sectionalism, as well, were
cauterized by patriotic heat. For all his pacifist sentiments, agrarian
hero William Jennings Bryan trained troops in Florida. He, like
most Americans, regarded Cuban independence as a morally righteous
cause and not a war of conquest. The future leader of urban, progressive America, young Theodore Roosevelt, a believer in America's
manifest destiny, helped lead the rambunctious Rough Riders in combat. Elderly ex-Confederate officers like Joseph Wheeler and Fitzhugh
Lee donned the once hated blue uniform and went to Cuba.[2]

The United States Army expanded from a force of 28,000 to 210,000
soldiers. Unable to handle the mobilization, the War Department
fell into such great confusion that troops stationed at home often
suffered as badly as those overseas. Because camps were improperly
sited and sanitation facilities were frequently inadequate, dysentery
and typhoid and Yellow fevers daily decimated the Army's ranks.
Of the nearly 200,000 conquering ex-servicemen who returned home
in the fall of 1898, thousands were in ill-health from the Army's poor
food as well as fevers. Many, too, were indigent, for they had had
no war-risk insurance and a private's pay had been set at $15 a
month. Substantial numbers of men found themselves almost penni-
less upon discharge.[3]

Whether or not they were poor, many ex-soldiers were emotionally adrift and sought security in association. America has always been a country of joiners as well as of garrulous patriots. The post-Civil War industrial expansion of the United States gradually developed a complex urban society with increased leisure time. Life seemed so complex, in fact, that Americans began to seek meaning and security by joining nationally organized special interest groups. Patriotic societies promoting nationalism, fraternalism and special benefits were especially popular and influential. For a generation after 1865 the Grand Army of the Republic (G.A.R.) managed to exact huge sums from the taxpayers and to dominate Republican politics. The G.A.R. was one of the by-products of urban social organization and the veterans of 1898 noted the financial largess extended to their elders and contrasted it with their own penury.[4]

America possessed great natural wealth in 1899, but little of that wealth accrued to the men who had so recently fought for their nation. Naturally, many soldiers felt that their services had been ignored by a selfish public. Some displayed a belligerent attitude about the war which frequently took the form of rhetorical bluster about the toughness of the Cuban or Philippine compaigns. On other occasions the veterans showed an envy of the G.A.R. Poor, edgy about his service, the war veteran felt he lacked job opportunities despite industrial expansion and the nation's indebtedness to him.[5]

Because the war had been so brief, the public could forget it; it did not affect the nation physically or emotionally as deeply as the Civil War had. Also, the techniques of public relations, which would serve a later generation of veterans so well, were crude in 1898. Public relations often involved personal vendettas between rival publishers, rather than functioning to advance the cause of a group. The frustrated Spanish War veteran cast about for means of making his voice heard. If he happened to be a farmer living in isolation, the chances were that he would never be heard at all. In the cities affairs were quite different. The G.A.R. was always strongest in urban areas and, despite the advanced age of its members, the organizational machinery still functioned. It obviously could not accept the new veterans, but it helped to serve as a guide. The newest generation of ex-soldiers looked at the old organization with increased interest.[6]

Economic considerations were not the only stimulus that brought about a new veterans' society. The rootlessness of a different America seemed to be having its effect. From Revolutionary days, hundreds of veteran and patriotic societies had flourished for purely pragmatic purposes. By 1898 new forces within the culture—mass immigration,

increased industrialism, the rise of organized labor, and the centraliza-
tion of capital—began to reshape the national scene. Many members
of the middle and lower middle classes felt psychologically displaced
in the new environment. The country was fast becoming a setting for
super organization where human relationships counted for little but
formal relations between large societies counted for much. With dis-
placement, the middle classes experienced insecurity and tension concerning the change in social status. Painful adjustments had to be
made and the old traditions and bonds of a predominantly Anglo-
Saxon culture seemed endangered by these alien social and economic
intrusions.[7]

Many men favorably recalled the war; in retrospect it appeared to
have represented a common experience overlaid with grandeur. That
grandeur symbolized a desire for an America in which their kind and
values predominated. If, in everyday practice, their lives were dry,
uninspired, and threatened by dimly comprehended forces, memories
of shared sufferings brought emotional security and became a readily
available compensation. The next step was an institutionalization of
such memories into a form that would guarantee them permanency.
A new ex-servicemen's organization.[8]

Technological, social, and economic forces were partially responsible,
therefore, for the formation of veterans' societies in 1898; but the
veterans' desire to band together and commemorate their war service
bore a remarkable resemblance to "cults of the dead."[9] Such cults
were common to other civilizations, they served the purpose of linking
the living community to that of the past. In regard to the Spanish
War veterans and their twentieth century successors, the desire to
maintain common experience was as important a reason for the creation of veterans' groups as any other. With only a few exceptions,
the nationally organized Spanish War veteran exhibited this particular
feeling longer than other veterans' organizations. The Spanish War
veterans' financial resources often were slim, and they never fully
comprehended the art of self-advertisement. Lack of money and
publicity continued to prevent them from erecting monuments to
their dead.[10]

Thirteen months after the outbreak of the war, the first of the
Spanish War veterans' societies appeared. Its start was symbolic,
for it grew out of the frustrations induced by an oversight. In May,
1899, the city of Washington, D.C., was the scene of a Jubilee Parade
which honored the successful creation of an overnight empire. The
order of the march had been set, the invitations to dignitaries had

been issued, and all was in readiness. Someone then noticed that
almost the only body of men not represented in the parade were those
who had fought in the war.[11] The committee sent for a Captain J.
Walker Mitchell, who managed to round up several hundred men for
the march. The organizers of the parade thus inadvertently were
responsible for the creation of the first 1898 war veterans' organization. After the festivities, some members of the forgotten contingent
decided to maintain their newly found friendship. They drew up
plans and, on September 8, 1899, the first national convention of the
Spanish War Veterans took place at Washington, D.C. General
J. Warren Keifer of Ohio narrowly defeated Theodore Roosevelt as
the elected commander-in-chief. If Roosevelt had been present, a
witness of the vote later said, the result would have been reversed.[12]

The first convention, in a suprising move, briefly flirted with race relations. When a council of administrators was chosen, the second man
elected was Colonel Hamilton H. Blount, a Negro and former commanding officer of a regiment of Negro immunes. The only Negro
present, his nomination was seconded by two southerners, Colonel
Frederick W. Cole, of Florida and Colonel James H. Tillman, of South
Carolina.[13]

Inclusion of a Negro in the society meant one thing to that generation and quite something else to a later one. The dominant theme of
the first convention was not racial equality, but the reconciliation of
North and South. The reunion meant removal of the old feud and
re-establishment of a non-sectional society. Tillman was the nephew
of Benjamin "Pitchfork Ben" Tillman, U.S. Senator from South Carolina and spokesman for the agrarian, segregationist Democrats in the
South. Before his arrival in Washington, the Senator had been noted
not only as an agrarian reformer but also as one of the leading pro-
ponents of racial segregation which had first appeared during the
1880's and 1890's in the South. The Colonel, who barely escaped
being court-martialed over an Army racial incident, subscribed fully
to his uncle's segregationist views.[14]

In 1899, when the younger Tillman seconded the Negro Blount,
it was hardly likely that he endorsed racial equality. No record exists
stating exactly why Tillman felt constrained to support Blount; perhaps he felt he should accept the predominant mood of the first convention. James Tillman was considered an ambitious, brilliant member
of the Tillman clan, with a great flair for politics. The nomination
was treated by an observer as a symbolic one. Whether or not Tillman
felt this way, too, or merely kept the soldier-vote in mind, is not

known. Superficially at least, Blount appeared to be the type of Negro that a Southerner conceivably might support. Blount was a field-grade officer and he possessed a good record. The Blount-Tillman incident, however, counted for no more than a sidelight of the convention. One of the society's founders thought that the adoption of an official uniform of blue and gray signified more proof than the Blount affair that sectionalism no longer existed.[15]

Early membership of the new society was heavily weighted with top-echelon regular officers such a Lieutenant-General Nelson A. Miles, Admiral George Dewey, and former Confederate generals, Joseph Wheeler and Fitzhugh Lee, as well as Theodore Roosevelt. Very few of these men fully participated in the society's affairs.[16] The group's members decided that honorary memberships should be prohibited except in the case of President William McKinley, who exerted a strong hold on the memory of the Spanish-American War veteran. For about a dozen years every national convention spoke in terms of pathetic eloquence about "the dear," "the glorious," "the fallen war leader." Undoubtedly, McKinley's social background made him a comforting and familiar figure to the U.S.W.V. But not even a bullet could transform the staid McKinley personality into a Lincoln-esque legend. A more probable explanation of his popularity was that if the G.A.R. possessed a martyr the veterans of Cuba were bound to emulate it.[17]

By 1902 the group officially called itself the National Army and Navy Spanish War Veterans. Permanent headquarters were established in the national capital and a female auxiliary was added. As late as 1903 there still appeared a belligerent attitude toward the G.A.R. One of the founders, Captain Mitchell, said that "some" regarded the war as trifling and that it would not produce an adequate supply of veterans to replace the G.A.R., but he noted that the association numbered about 135,000 in 1903 and that another group, the Spanish-American War Veterans, with 25,000 members was about to amalgamate with the larger organization.[18] The fusion took place on April 18, 1904, when the Spanish War Veterans, the Spanish-American War Veterans and the Service Men of the Spanish War were united into one body called the United Spanish War Veterans (U.S.W.V.). In 1907 the Massachusetts Legion of Spanish War Veterans joined the U.S.W.V. and in 1908 the Veteran Army of the Philippines entered the ranks as well. In addition, veterans of the American relief expedition during the 1901 Boxer Rebellion were admitted. The consolidation was a wise decision. Scattered efforts and divided membership could not, the U.S.W.V. admitted later, secure the objectives for which they were organized.[19]

The preamble to the U.S.W.V. constitution revealed the spirit and aims of the organization. The United Veterans felt that the war was conceived and executed in a sublime spirit of unselfishness and sacrifice, The Philippines' insurrection had been incidental and so had the American relief expedition to China in 1901. What had been important in 1898 was that peoples suffering under misrule and tyranny were given independence. Victory in Cuba and in the Pacific had been glorious.[20] America's part in the Boxer Rebellion and the conquest of the Philippines "emphasized the unselfishness of our aims and added prestige to our arms," and the entire era had been an inspiring chapter in the nation's military history. The period from April 21, 1898 to July 4, 1902 was one that "was emblematic of sacrifice and devotion to the principles of liberty, equal rights and justice to all mankind, and one which must ever act as a stimulus to patriotic endeavor in the years to come."[21]

The magnitude of the victory made the United States known and respected the world over, the U.S.W.V. realized. Sectional lines at home were obliterated, the nation was welded together and permeated with a renewed spirit of national pride. In addition, humanity pervaded all sections of our Republic. When the war ended, however, its memories needed to be perpetuated and those comrades who answered the last call were to be honored. Patriotism and recognition of war service to the survivors were twin objectives, as well as aid for impecunious comrades and their dependents.[22] In order to accomplish this, veterans would have to carry into the less spectacular walks of life the same spirit of sacrifice that they had so recently exhibited. Finally, the veterans were told to exert influence on the national government to provide adequate national defense. All this, the U.S.W.V. stated, called for a national organization whose members would be pledged "to promote the principles of Freedom, Patriotism and Humanity."[23]

The interesting aspect of the preamble was the incorporation of the Spanish veterans' ideals into its constitution and, later, into practice. The organization listed nine primary objects or aims in its constitution: fraternal bonds: honor of the dead and preservation of their graves; assistance to distressed members and their families; perpetuation of war memories; promotion of the veterans' best interests; inculcation of democratic principles and reverence for American institutions; and finally, maintenance of a large defense force, education of the people in defense affairs and help for the services in the event of another war.[24]

Patriotism was listed as the sixth goal. In practice the U.S.W.V. adhered to its goals in very much the same order as they were written in 1904. In all its history, patriotism, while fundamental to the society, has never been put on a highly organized or institutionalized basis. On those occasions when it has, almost always the event has revolved around a memorial service for the dead or the retelling of a wartime experience. Thoughout its history the U.S.W.V. has kept its eyes rooted on the years from 1898 to 1902.[25]

There was no doubt that the veterans felt that patriotism was important and that it needed stimulus. The constitution's use of the word "inculcate" indicated that some persons felt more Americans needed patriotic instruction. The U.S.W.V. was, of course, quite typical of its age and class in regard to patriotism. A highly evangelical or missionary atmosphere characterized its founding and persisted during its subsequent history. It resolved to "preach" the spirit of patriotism; it fought "America's first war for humanity"; strength was based upon religion, and the veterans were likened to "Crusaders" who sacrificed themselves in a war against tyranny and its attendant immorality.[26]

In stressing the theme of reunion at their first convention, the organization's members exhibited a desire to return to a unity they thought had existed prior to 1861. Healing the sectional wound would renew the national spirit of the early republic, whose good will should be maintained within the country as one of its cherished principles.[27] They also thought that the nation's recently recovered unity might be endangered by new forces in the society. In particular, the group feared Eastern and Southern European immigration, and later supported its restriction.[28] The recently arrived immigrants who had swarmed into the eastern cities knew little if anything of American history and customs. Furthermore, it seemed they did not care to know and this fact bothered the veterans.[29]

The image of America, as the brotherhood saw it, was not a specific one but it was representative of the one held by many Americans in the years before the First World War. It consisted of traditional, middle-class values: law, order, respect for magistrates, support of religion and loyalty. Mixed in with these conventional beliefs was a tenet of the urban progressive reformism which manifested itself nationally during the veterans' early years. Members sensed a need "to encourage honor and purity in public affairs" while the National

Commandary also urged "unceasing battle for right" in municipal government. Judged by its own records, it appears that the U.S.W.V., in its point of origin, in much of its social composition, and in its officially expressed views on the American image, was a part of the urban segment of the progressive movement. One of the distinguishing marks of many of these progressives was their predilection for jingoism, a choice definitely not shared by all progressive reformers. This strident patriotism was a partial reaction to the drab but uncertain new civilization in which the middle-class progressive was forced to live. It was the age of Richard Harding Davis and Rudyard Kipling; an age of exacting heroism and manly, militant glory.[30]

The U.S.W.V. concept of patriotism, when compared to those of later ex-soldiers' groups, seems less formal, perhaps because patriotism before World War I had not been fully institutionalized. The pledge of allegiance had been but recently written. "The Star Spangled Banner" was not to become an official anthem until 1931. Frequently, as at the flag raising ceremony over Santiago de Cuba in 1898, a band played "Hail Columbia." On the eve of the war with Spain there had been some discussion of having every public school in the country decorated by a flag. Few civilians saluted the flag, although an intensive flag cult had been started earlier by the G.A.R. Even the armed forces were not always punctilious about ritual. In September, 1899, when President McKinley inspected the United States Navy's North Atlantic Squadron, none of the ships bothered to carry a presidential flag. Inexplicably, a passing ferryboat was reported as rescuing the embarrassed sailors. The ferry's captain somehow managed to produce a presidential pennant.[31]

So it appeared that while Americans were intensely nationalistic in the years before World War I, they had not yet entangled patriotism in a mass of ritual. Such ritual would come, but what patriotic practices existed came from the G.A.R.[32] Since patriotism had not yet been institutionalized, the United Spanish War Veterans regarded it and its spirit in a way quite different from that of later generations of veterans. The spirit of America to the Spanish War veterans was a belief in conventional middle-class values. Such concepts were written in the preamble and constitution of the organization.

In 1894, young Theodore Roosevelt, who also had been concerned with the spirit of America, enunciated one of his earliest ideas on the subject. He was bothered by the new America he saw emerging. Although he accepted the facts of a changed environment, he wished native Americans, particularly of the middle classes, to transfer the

blessings of the old society to the new. The new United States and
all its recent members, Roosevelt insisted, should be "Americanized."
"But I wish to be distinctly understood . . . Americanism is a question of spirit, conviction, and purpose, not of creed or birthplace." [33]
Roosevelt's words and convictions applied to such organization as the
U.S.W.V.; if the society appeared to be inarticulate on the spirit
of Americanism in its early years it was because it did not have to
be specific. Conventional as the words of the preamble were, they
evoked immediate comprehension and understanding by the members.
These were the concepts that the ex-servicemen had always known.

There was another aspect to the idea of Americanism. Members
have always been proud to point out that theirs is "the only one
hundred per cent volunteer army the Country ever had." [34] Initially
the veterans were not overly concerned with the trappings of patriotism because their service was proof alone of Americanism. "We
fought," the U.S.W.V., has said proudly, "with poor equipment, poor
food and antiquated guns." As the years rolled on and new veterans'
groups formed, the United Veterans subscribed in some degree to a
new type of patriotism, but they never have lost their early feeling
that service in the swamps was the real badge of the American spirit.
Half a century after the U.S.W.V. was founded, a member stated
that the society "has for many years been . . . recognized for its
Americanism work as every man who served . . . volunteered his
services and none were drafted." [35]

If the U.S.W.V.'s primary purpose was perpetuation of the memories
of American crusaders, other Spanish War veterans were more pragmatic. Their story was summarized years later by the cry, "We are
those who refused to be forgotten!" In Columbus, Ohio during the
year 1899, James Romanis, a veteran of the Cuban war, was disturbed
when he "saw his suffering comrades going to the poor house and dying
in squalor." On the night of September 29, 1899, Romanis and twelve
friends met in the back room of a tailoring shop in Columbus where,
according to official legend, they discussed the plight of the returned
men. A club was organized named the American Veterans of Foreign
Service and membership was limited to those who had served overseas. All members were pledged "to help one another and to work for
the benefit of our country and for the men who fight for this nation."
The aim was couched in general terms but the implication was clear:
the returned soldier intended to organize for purposes of material and
economic security. [36]

The records of the Columbus meeting bristle with the resentment felt by Romanis and his friends. The accounts describe the veterans as prematurely aged by the ravages of tropical fever, bad food and medical neglect. They were unhappy as civilians; when they returned home, they felt, they received little attention. Many, it was said, were desperately ill and could not work steadily. Few government hospitals existed and no financial assistance was available. "The plain fact was that no one cared what happened to them . . . It was a picture of deplorable neglect." [37]

In Denver, Colorado, another group of Spanish War veterans held a similar meeting. Most of these men, who met on December 1, 1899, had served in the Philippines' campaign; they elected as their leader General Irving Hale. The talk was much the same and the announced goals appeared to be in complete harmony with those of the Ohio group and the U.S.W.V. They called themselves the Colorado Society of the Army of the Philippines. They pledged themselves to loyalty to the United States and to the principles of "comradeship, perpetuation of the memory of departed comrades, and assistance to their widows." The group then introduced a clause into its charter which has proven to be one of the most ambivalent features of the work of patriotic societies. They promised to foster "true patriotism" and to extend "the institutions of American freedom." Precisely what "true patriotism" was the Philippine veterans neglected to say. [38]

Neither of the two groups made much headway between 1900 and the eve of the First World War. Other units were organized in industrialized areas of Pennsylvania, but outside of local aid to fellow members and social activities, the newest organizations did not impress themselves upon the public consciousness. In 1913 the Ohio, Colorado, and Pennsylvania groups joined together into one society named the Veterans of Foreign Wars of the United States (V.F.W.). To be eligible, a man had to have served overseas and, like the U.S.W.V., it was open to all overseas veterans regardless of rank held. [39]

Although the V.F.W. did not attract much publicity during its early years, it elaborated its aims, designed an emblem, and attempted to organize itself on a truly national scale. The stated purpose of the V.F.W. was to be fraternal, patriotic, historical, and educational. The old phrase from the Colorado charter concerning "true patriotism" reappeared in the new organization's list of aims and, as before, the exact meaning or a definition of the term was missing. [40]

The V.F.W. chose a "crusader" motif for its emblem. Just as the U.S.W.V. had thought of itself as a group of Christians fighting the infidel, so did the V.F.W. Their official badge became the "Cross of

Malta." The organization stated that this selection was entirely
symbolic and that the emblem originally came from the Knights of St.
John, "the world's first great brotherhood of men who fought to free
the oppressed and administer to the sick and needy." V.F.W.'s members were "like the original Crusaders," for they also pledged themselves to fight for the freedom of mankind and to administer to the less
fortunate. A modern, crusading comrade, it was explained, ful-
filled his vows by "giving aid to worthy comrades and helping their
windows and orphans." In addition, the V.F.W. knight was adjured
to eternal defense of every man's right to "life, liberty and the pursuit
of happiness." The terms and phraseology were familiar and traditional. They also awaited further enunciation and clarification.[41]

In 1913, on the eve of a general European war, many Spanish-
American War veterans, in and out of organized groups, feared for
America's military unpreparedness. The U.S.W.V. especially recommended a strong military reserve. Its main emphasis lay in a traditional American fighting force composed of a strong navy, a small
regular army, and a large militia of reserve.[42] By 1914 the Spanish
War veterans' societies concentrated on charity for their poor members, strengthened fraternal bonds, and cared for graves and memor-
ials. They resembled the welter of service organizations so dear to
the heart of middle-class America. Intense patriots they were, but not
as yet militant in an organized sense.

In seeking aid for veterans, the U.S.W.V. was less blatant than other
groups. It managed to give the impression that it regarded the
treatment of Spanish War veterans more in sorrow than anger. The
V.F.W. was not as reticent; it expressed more bitterness than the
U.S.W.V. over the treatment of veterans. Initially the voices of both
groups were muted by organizational growing pains and local problems. Both were part of the progressive mosaic in urban areas; both
were fervently moral and evangelical about the spread of American
social and national institutions, and both strongly upheld middle-
class values. If the members of the U.S.W.V. and the V.F.W. felt
they had attained security through organization, they needed such
feelings. The next forty years would see assaults upon the values
and institutions the veterans cherished. The Spanish-American War
veterans, aided by newer patriotic societies, met the attacks. Their
method of defense, however, was to disquiet other groups of Americans.
To many citizens it seemed that organized veterans' groups employed
authoritarian measures in the preservation of liberty.[43]

CHAPTER III

TWO LEGIONS

The American Legion is the largest and most popular of the modern veterans' organizations. It is to this century, in its own eyes at least, what the Grand Army of the Republic was to nineteenth century America.

Members of the Legion have been represented in every one of our wars since 1917 and a few of its eldest comrades even fought in 1898 as well as in World War I. Quite naturally, in view of such a record and within its own patriotic context, the Legion feels that its position is pre-eminent as the conservator and defender of national idealism. Such a role is buttressed in a variety of ways, but one of the main and skillfully employed tactics is identification with the public. A large membership and excellent community service programs are the usual means used to obtain the goal.

Aside from such considerations, there are elements of mysticism involved in the over-all attempt to unite the Legion, the people and the concept of the nation-state. One of the forms has been the creation of legends about how the martial fraternity sprang spontaneously into being from the ranks of all classes of soldiers who served the country. Supposedly, such instinctive behavior symbolizes a traditionally American democratic version of the *volksgeist* or the folk spirit. This notion underscores the essentially indigenous nature of the fighting men's brotherhood. Initially the Legion made a great pretense of emphasizing this theory of its creation, but its antagonists during the twenties and thirties happily demolished such contentions by proving that the General Headquarters of the American Expeditionary Force offered high-level assistance at its birth. Evidence exists, moreover, that its origins even pre-date 1918. Official policy on the group's founding today is relatively factual and much less ingenuous than it once was, but in a vague fashion it still plays upon the old theme with a lighter touch. The society has never tried to hide its exact beginnings despite charges to the contrary. The record is there; it simply is ignored. The present American Legion was formally incorporated in 1919, but it truly was originated in the period 1914-1915.

Although they had always been on the world stage, most Americans chose to ignore the fact and in 1914 were only beginning to emerge from their self-created sense of isolationism. When war broke out in Europe the public generally appeared unable to grasp the issues or their stake in the outcome. Militarily speaking, the United States was a second-class power with a good navy but an inadequate army. This fact did not bother too many citizens, most of whom apparently assumed that neutrality best served the national interest. Moreover, the leaders of the period for the most part failed to acquaint the public with the realities of international politics. The United States eventually entered the war, but in the view of several contemporary historians the nation blundered into the conflict for unrealistic reasons.[1]

The war upset the European balance of power that had benefited America since the 1815 Congress of Vienna. German submarines almost shattered British control of the seas, which brought a crisis in German-American relations in 1915. President Wilson and many Americans wished to stay neutral, but they also wished to defend American rights on the seas. The United States was caught between German submarine policy and the British blockade of the Central Powers. Whichever way America turned, she offended someone and was offended in turn. The Wilson Administration appeared to switch policies several times, and Wilson sometimes refused to explain his reasons for the changes. The most notable instance of such a refusal occurred over the issue of armed merchant vessels.[2]

The German government tried a policy of unrestricted U-boat warfare against unarmed vessels but the British armed their ships and stood firm despite heavy losses. Public opinion in the United States hardened in its pro-Allied sentiments as some American lives were lost in the sinkings. Wilson was sure that Americans did not wish to go to war over the submarine issue but at the same time, the maritime policies of Germany and Britain seemed to dictate American foreign policy. To solve this dilemma Wilson secretly decided to intervene and, with close Allied co-operation, force Germany to discuss peace. His purpose seems to have been an attempt to restore the balance of power. American military intervention was to be a last resort. Concurrent with his hidden peace moves, Wilson suggested publicly that the British disarm their merchant ships and warned that America would treat armed vessels as auxiliary cruisers. The British refused, and the Germans announced the intention of sinking all armed merchantmen without warning. The American government stated that it would hold Germany to strict account in such a case.

Democrats in Congress worriedly regarded the government's action as a reversal of policy that might lead to war. Wilson refused to back down or explain his seeming shift of plans for he could not do so without exposing his plans for a peace settlement.[3]

When the U-boat crisis awakened the American people, it dawned on many that force alone was replacing reason as the arbiter in international conflicts. In this respect America appeared powerless, for the country was too weak militarily to defend itself or exert power overseas. Suddenly, as is the American wont, segments of the populace became raucously preoccupied with preparedness. Both of the Spanish war societies had long been pledged to the maintenance of a strong national defense. One member of the U.S.W.V.—Theodore Roosevelt, hyper-nationalist, romantic militarist and apostle of preparedness—marshalled more notoriety than the rest of his comrades. Although his career was studded by a superficial militarism, Roosevelt was genuinely concerned about America's safety. When the Germans sank the British Cunard Liner, Lusitania, in 1915, T.R. demanded that Wilson take militant steps in reprisal.[4]

Roosevelt was one of those men who believed that force alone made sense to the Germans. As some historians have noted, he curiously resembled the Kaiser in his concept of military power. Primarily Roosevelt loved the qualities of discipline, organization and, above all, vibrant patriotism often associated with militarism. He considered America too weak, however, to bend Germany to her will. Accompanied by others, he lectured passionately and wrote strongly about the state of American unpreparedness during 1915. The preparedness campaign threatened to become a political issue in the 1916 presidential contest but, respected as Roosevelt was, he represented a minority point of view. Most Americans felt armaments increased the chances of involvement. The former President needed help on his campaign; it came from Major General Leonard Wood, an old friend and comrade of Cuban days.[5]

A number of preparedness organizations (the National Security League and the American Defense Society) were springing up in 1914-1915. At first the Wilson administration appeared undecided about the preparedness issue. Although Wilson was not a pacifist, he clearly distrusted militarism and professional soldiers as did many members of the Democratic party in Congress. Officers of the regular military establishment who preached preparedness were regarded with suspicion by groups within the government. As a result, many soldiers publicly kept silent on the preparedness issue. General

Leonard Wood, however, did not feel constraint in speaking out
publicly on defense matters. Wood regarded the preparedness problem as a question of morality. The fundamental issue, as Wood saw
it, was the preservation of American national honor, and this clearly
constituted a moral problem. In 1915 Wood was Commanding
General of the Army's Department of the East. His headquarters,
it was noted, were located on Governor's Island, New York, con-
veniently near the metropolitan press.[6]

One day in January, 1915, Wood gave a talk at the New York City
Harvard Club. His talk, as usual, centered around his views on the
state of American unpreparedness. The General "supplied" his
friends with data showing the woeful state of our arms, and the need
for military muscle. Someone asked Wood if he could not do something about starting training camps. According to one account, "the
idea took root." Wood became "the patron saint," the "guide," and
the inspiration" of defense societies. Surreptitiously, Wood began to
deal with various groups. One society wished to organize an unofficial reserve consisting of men who possessed prior military training
or were skilled technicians. Wood reached this group through his
aide-de-camp, Captain Gordon Johnston, and a former army officer,
Doctor J. E. Hausmann. Wood told Roosevelt of the proposed organization, self styled The American Legion.[7]

On February 22, 1915, Roosevelt felt moved to inform the Legion
that he thought its formation was an excellent idea. He described
himself as sympathetic to its avowed purpose and announced, "I
and my sons will gladly become members." Roosevelt added that he
wanted no war, but that he was certain that the surest way to avert
war was to be prepared. He then expressed his romantic hope that if
war came he would be granted permission to raise a division of cavalry
like the old Rough Riders. The division would consist of nine regiments of horse and its ranks "would largely be filled by men of the
Legion." [8]

The idea of the Legion publicly appeared a few days later at the end
of February in a magazine called *Adventure*. In a column under the
heading of "Camp Fire," the rough outlines of a civilian reserve "a
legion of adventurers," were sketched. Wartime service was the primary purpose of the Legion; there would be no obligations made upon
it in peacetime.[9] On March 1, 1915, Dr. Hausmann and Captain
Johnston announced the Legion's formal debut. The Legion would
not promote militarism, they said, and there would be but "small place
in its ranks for hyphenated Americans" who owed a double allegiance.[10]

On March 5, 1915, the American Legion was incorporated in New York City. The incorporation articles stated that the object of the organization was to organize American citizens to serve the country in time of war. By way of expressing their patriotism members were to honor and wear an insignia of red, white and blue. When Justice Edward J. Gavegan indicated that he felt its purpose was not stated clearly enough, the Legion's attorney, E. Ormonde Power, promptly inserted the words "to promote patriotism"—whereupon Justice Gavegan signed the incorporating certificate. In addition to Power's signature, the incorporation papers bore the names of Alexander M. White, Julien T. Davies, Jr., Arthur S. Hoffman and Theodore Roosevelt, Jr., from or near the metropolitan area of New York City.[11]

Newsmen asked Dr. Hausmann where the idea had originated. Hausmann related a romantic tale about a young American named E. D. Cook, who had left the United States presumably to join one of the European armies. Cook had providentially mailed a letter to the magazine editor of *Adventure* before sailing and in it had proposed a legion of adventurers to serve the country in warfare. The editor, Arthur Sullivant Hoffman, laid the plans before General Wood. The latter had approved of them, said Hausmann, as a valuable movement in the direction of preparedness. Hausmann pointed out that there were exactly eighteen men in the National Reserve. He said nothing of Cook's fate.[12]

At the same time Hausmann and Johnston made their announcement, Roosevelt publicly approved of the Legion. Not only did T.R. approve, but he accepted appointment to the executive council of the group. The council was distinguished; other members included William Howard Taft, Joseph McGavock Dickinson, Luke E. Wright, Henry L. Stimson, George Meyer, Truman H. Newberry, and Elihu Root—all former Secretaries of War or Navy.[13]

On three fronts the effect of the new organization was immediate and explosive. Pacifists demanded that the sinister link between such civilian militarists and the Regular Army be revealed.[14] In Washington the War Department began an investigation, but the press generally felt the formation of a reserve, even a privately sponsored one, was a sound idea.[15]

The Wilson administration realized that Roosevelt's name on the masthead of a national preparedness society gave the Republicans an issue and a sounding board in the 1916 elections. Secretary of War Lindley Miller Garrison and Secretary of the Navy Josephus

Daniels sent inquiries. Describing the communication from Garrison
as "excited", Wood denied that the organization was militaristic. He
was only interested in a patriotic movement whose sole purpose was
to bolster national defense.[16] But in some respects Wood did his
old comrade, Roosevelt, a disservice. Any organization with T.R.'s
name on it automatically became identified with politics. Wood petu-
lantly tried to explain to the administration that Roosevelt was only a
volunteer, that the Legion was not conducting propaganda, and that
it only existed as a card index in case of emergency.[17] Much of this
explanation appeared as sophistry on Wood's part. A close friend of
Wood was forced to admit that Wilson's suspicions were human
ones in view of Roosevelt's known antagonism to the national
administration and Wood's Republican leanings. Wood, however,
said that Wilson showed "a disturbing blindness" to the fact that in
a crisis "devotion to country might predominate over personal
ambition." [18]

Wood's Republican affiliations gave him a political posture. Quite
ingenuously, his supporters admitted that the public furor over his
part in creating the Legion gained significance in the light of military
discipline. Four days before the Legion's organization, Wood received a general order from Garrison which prohibited all members
of the army from publicly discussing defense matters. The order
was to no avail. The General "knew" that the Secretary of War
was ardent in the preparedness cause. He "did not take the order
seriously"; instead, he "threw himself on the mercy" of reporters and
"went ahead." [19]

Almost immediately after the public announcement of the Legion's
formation, Roosevelt said that he hoped to get both Republicans and
Democrats on the Council. He even wanted Secretary Garrison, but
conceded that he realized such a move was impossible. The Legion
was only a registry for the government's use, he emphasized. The
administration was supposed to do this itself, the irate former President insisted, but "probably never will." When the government
failed to act it was wrong for individuals not to take action.[20] Roosevelt
then stated that he did not wish to be made the chairman of the Executive Council, for "it will be utterly impossible to persuade people
that there is not something political in it." But Roosevelt, was
quickly compromised by Wood. There was nothing political about the
Legion, Wood told Garrison; according to one journal Wood swore
that Roosevelt never communicated with him about the Legion.
Actually, Roosevelt's public endorsement of the Legion on February

22, 1915 had been made in response to a personal letter from the Legion, whose military adviser was Wood's aide, Captain Johnston. Even if Wood had not written to Roosevelt directly, his personal views were known to the former Chief Executive. Wood was more than insubordinate. Whatever good he may have felt he had done on the country's behalf by ignoring orders, such good was mitigated by the Wood-Roosevelt relationship. This connection was bound to antagonize Wilson. Wood was either politically obtuse or he tried to fashion a political plank for the Republicans. At the same time he forced the preparedness issue onto Wilson in a manner the President was unable to ignore.[21]

The public response was, at first, satisfactory. Wood reported that within the first week a thousand volunteers signed applications. The New York *Herald* (Independent) estimated that by June, 1915, 50,000 men were to be enrolled. The *Herald* said that three hundred thousand members was the goal and pointed out that there was not "a tinge of politics" connected with the Legion. The New York *American* (Independent) admonished Secretary Garrison not to give in to "sentimental pacifists" by disciplining Wood. What Garrison should do, said the paper, was to give consideration to such a reserve. The *Outlook* scolded members of the League to Limit Armaments who made haste to condemn the Legion without having realized that the Legion "was not in any sense" a military organization.[22] For several months Roosevelt retained his singularly romantic concept of the Legion and its role. In July, 1915, he wrote to an in-law and said that if it was necessary to use the Legion in war, he was ready to get his relative in. He warned his correspondent, though, "personally . . . I do not believe that this Administration can be kicked into war . . ."[23]

By the following November, Wilson presented his preparedness program to the Congress and the resultant fight revealed two things of consequence. Despite the prospect of war, there was a violent reaction against preparedness on the part of many persons which illustrated that pacifist sentiment was still strong in the country. It also showed that such organizations as the American Legion, the National Security League, and the National Defense Society, were in a minority within the country in general. Their formation and membership, as in the Legion's case, came from the urban areas.[24] By 1916 American defense orders were placed with industry and real rearmament began. An emergent military machine cut the ground from under the American Legion and it subsided into a dormant state. The War Department ignored the organization and the name lived on only in the minds of a few.[25]

The furor over the 1915 Legion helped dramatize American military unpreparedness. It might have aided the plans of those who wished to enlarge the military establishment. Compared to the role played by German U-boats, however, its effect in strengthening American arms was minor. The preparedness society, however, left two bequests. The first legacy was the name American Legion. Members of the Roosevelt family and former members of the 1915 Legion were extremely active in the founding of a new Legion which arose at General Headquarters (G.H.Q.) in 1918. There also was the gift of Roosevelt's spirit of rambunctious, militant nationalism. It was bequeathed to a new American Legion, and its effects were lasting.[26]

When the United States entered the war in the spring of 1917, Americans, as the Calvinist-President fearfully forecast, embraced intolerance as a necessity. Not the least of the tragedies of Woodrow Wilson was that he marshalled the very forces of illiberalism he despised so deeply. Once more an American phenomenon, the spirit of missionary morality on democracy's behalf, was loosed upon the world. To insure peace and guarantee the "extensions of American institutions," it was necessary to use ultimate and terrible forces. The United States marched forth on a moral crusade to make the world safe for democracy.[27]

Emotionalism, however, was hard to sustain and with the war's end a reaction began to seep through the public at home and through the ranks of the American Expeditionary Force (A.E.F.). Between November 11, 1918 and late December, 1919, some four million men who had comprised the United States military forces during the First World War were discharged. In Germany, 20,000 Americans remained on occupation duty. Judged by the postwar literary efforts of ex-servicemen, such as John Dos Passos, Ernest Hemingway and others, few found anything glamorous or idealistic in their service period. The ex-soldiers may have hated military service, but the emotional patriotism of the war years lifted them to a place of eminence. With peace, however, the doughboy was forced to vacate this position and face an uncertain future. A certain loss of security was inevitable. Around these frustrations clung the passions of war-hate and disgust, plus distrust of things foreign. A certain percentage of veterans, like others before them, felt that they had been tried by the fires of war and that they were, therefore, in a special position to know what life in America truly meant. Drawing upon the emotional-

ism generated by the war, various groups of veterans assigned themselves the task of defining national patriotism.[28]

One factor that helped to galvanize the concept of national patriotism was the great mobilization of the First World War. Gone forever,
in practice, was the old belief that America's youth could "spring to
arms" overnight. The civilian world, no less than the doughboy's,
was regimented for the national state. In 1898, it had still been
possible for the New York Seventh Regiment of the state guard to
refuse service in the Spanish-American War, the excuse being that
the regiment resented the undue influence of West Pointers. Twenty
years later all American manpower, and some female power as well,
was mobilized. An official propaganda agency effectively convinced
the public of the nobility of the United States; civilians with missionary zeal "did their part for Uncle Sam," and literally millions of
young men were first introduced to an organized, military ritual
greatly expanded since 1898. Indeed it was partially because of such
ceremonies that many ex-servicemen would join veterans' associations,
for psychologically they symbolized a period of communal dedication.[29]

The country to which the returned veteran addressed himself was
a muddled one. The peak of the progressive reform movement
had been reached with the signing of the Armistice; "The Great Crusade" was over and progressivism ebbed from the national consciousness. The reaction was immediate and bitter. Rapid demobilization cast millions of soldiers into labor markets that were unable to
absorb them readily. American labor was restless and a rash of
strikes broke out shortly after the Armistice. The American people,
conditioned by war patriotism, looked upon these disputes as contrary
to the public interest. In one sense the public was frustrated because
the term "unpatriotic" began to lose its significance with the end of
combat operations.[30]

Returning veterans and the civilians at home, spurred by war-time
emotionalism, fell prey to the fears engendered by the spread of European Bolshevism. The convulsions of civil war, seizure of private
property, wholesale extinction of classes, and the conspiratorial nature
of world-wide revolution which accompanied Communist expansion
understandably scared the citizens of the United States. The middle
classes were especially terrified because the Bolshevists were pledged to
eradicate them in particular.[31] Communism, it turned out, also offered
some public officials in this country a convenient symbol upon which
to vent their wrath and also gain publicity. Mayor Ole Hanson of
Seattle, Washington, announced that the Seattle general strike of

February, 1919 was the work of Bolshevists acting through the International Workers of the World (I.W.W.). For Hanson there was no middle ground concerning Bolshevism; Americans should stand up and be counted. Either an American was for his country or he was against it; either he was for the I.W.W. or against it.[32] The feeling that labor forces were infected by Bolshevism was heightened by an even more serious general strike in May, 1919, at Winnepeg, Canada. In the United States, the steel strike and the Boston police strike added to the fear and uncertainty of the public.[33]

When New York postal authorities discovered sixteen bombs in the mails addressed to various prominent persons, public wrath and fears reached unscaled heights. Mayor Hanson, be it noted, was not passed up during the wave of bomb scares that swept the nation during the 1919-1920 period; in April, 1919, he, too, found a bomb in his mail. Speaking of the anarchists and Bolsheviks allegedly connected with the bomb plots, Hanson graphically described his feelings to some veterans: "The soldiers and sailors who love this land far outnumber that 'cootie' crew who would wreck it. Let us go over the top together and clean them up. Let us sign no armistice. Our terms: Deportation, Incarceration, Annihilation!"[34]

Such exciting but violent and combustible accolades reached their zenith with the bombing of United States Attorney General Palmer's house in Washington, D.C. and the sensational bombing of Wall Street on September 16, 1920. Because of the dramatic nature of these bombings, the small number of anarchists then in the country seemed magnified. The fact that the radicals were split and constituted scant menace meant little to most Americans.[35]

Overseas, meanwhile, the A.E.F. stirred restlessly with far too much time on its hands. Officers apprehensively watched troop morale plummet as they heard tales of anarchists, Marxists, and radicals in general. The General Headquarters of the A.E.F. became the scene of much uneasiness during the winter of 1918-1919. People back home, noting the dip in A.E.F. morale wondered whether or not the returning doughboys, if infected by Marxism, might not associate with the I.W.W.[36]

Confusion and myth surround the birth of what was to become the new American Legion. For years the new Legion insisted that its origin was "spontaneous." One romantic tale recounted how Lieutenant Colonel Theodore Roosevelt, Jr., first conceived the idea and passed it on to Sergeant William Patterson in 1918. Both were recovering from wounds received from the Aisne-Marne battle when the discussion took place. Patterson was later killed but Roosevelt, while still hospitalized, talked the idea over with others.[37]

In actuality, General Pershing called selected officers from various units in France to discuss the problem of bad morale and Bolshevism. In January, 1919, Lieutenant Colonel George A. White, G.H.Q., met with Roosevelt and the two discussed the sad state of affairs. Roosevelt suggested the remedy of a veterans' group within the A.E.F. When the troops returned home, the organization would enroll all men who had served honorably in the war. The purpose was to harness the "restless energy" of the servicemen and preserve the unity of fighting men during the war. The fruits of victory would thus be "perpetuated." White gave Roosevelt full credit, although the latter deliberately underplayed his role in the years to come.[38]

Roosevelt told White that he had, indeed, thought of a new veterans' society while hospitalized. There is no reason to doubt Roosevelt. His account, in view of the 1915 Legion, cleared General Pershing from the charge of being the second Legion's father. Such accusations were once made and other charges were also leveled at the ubiquitous Leonard Wood as its originator; however much Wood may have had to do with the 1915 Legion, he was not overtly connected with the new one. Theodore Roosevelt, Jr. suggested the idea to key G.H.Q. personnel and there was a strong suspicion that he helped Pershing select the officers who assembled at Paris. Wood and Pershing disliked one another and Pershing was not beholden to much that Wood suggested. Wood made one visit to G.H.Q. and found the atmosphere "oppressive." Pershing's staff, however, contained many who knew and admired Wood. It was these latter that the younger Theodore Roosevelt approached.[39]

On the night of February 15, 1919, Roosevelt's famous dinner for the twenty officers took place. He told his comrades of his plans for a new veterans' organization. The majority of men at the dinner were from the eastern part of the United States. The few from the Midwest and the Far West were from urban areas within their respective states. No one from the deep South, which was predominantly rural, was there. Lieutenant Colonel Bennett C. Clark, Jr., son of the Speaker of the House, Bennett Champ Clark, Missouri Democrat, attended. Four members of the 1915 American Legion, in addition to Roosevelt, were also present. They were Colonel William J. Donovan, Lieutenant Colonel David M. Goodrich, Captain Ogden L. Mills, and Colonel R. C. Stebbins. All were from the New York City area. In addition, Major D. D. Drain and Henry L. Lindsley, also members of the 1915 Legion, were to attain prominence in the new American Legion. Although its creators were from the cities, in time the society would find its major strength in rural America. Roosevelt gave the new organization no name. Why he did not has caused much speculation among those who interested themselves in the Legion's creation. *Adventure Magazine's* former editor, Arthur Hoffman, wrote in 1934 that he gladly had given written consent for the transfer of the 1915 Legion's name to the newer society. Conceivably Roosevelt did not wish to rake up the political partisanship connected with the earlier group.[40]

Immediately after the Paris dinner, Colonel White managed to tour all the units of the A.E.F. Officially, G.H.Q. appeared to take little notice of his travels, but a Legion historian recounted in 1923 how White had used government gasoline and vehicles for his trip. White acquainted members of the A.E.F. with the idea of a veterans' society. Roosevelt, meanwhile, rushed home to organize the veterans who had remained in this country. Publicity about the new Legion in the United States was meager as late as March, 1919.[41]

The Paris caucus of the American Legion met in March, 1919. In attendance were such diverse personalities as Colonel Bennett Champ Clark, Jr., Sergeant Alvin C. York, America's most decorated war hero, and a rather puzzled private named Harold W. Ross, who wandered into the caucus more by mistake than anything else. Later he edited a magazine for the Legion. Another delegate was a porcine young man named Alexander Woolcott of the United States Army Medical Corps. When names for the new group were suggested, Woolcott objected to the title that was adopted. It smelled too much of "silk-stocking," he announced. Possibly he had reference to the 1915 Legion which may further explain Roosevelt's earlier personal reluctance in suggesting the title to his Paris dinner companions. Woolcott's objection nettled another delegate who called the future drama critic "a fat medico" and favorably likened the new American Legion to the exotic French Foreign Legion. Feelings ran high.[42]

In May of the same year, at St. Louis, Missouri, the second caucus met and agreed to adopt the same name as the overseas branch. It was believed by some that the new Legion would serve as an organization for the political future of Theodore Roosevelt, Jr. For that very reason, and possibly because he remembered the suspicion toward the old Legion, Roosevelt turned the leadership of the caucus down. The refusal was made with great difficulty, for the self-effacing Roosevelt was clearly the most popular leader. Organizational plans progressed and, on September 16, 1919, the United States Congress granted a charter making the "American Legion a corporation of the United States." [43]

There was some discussion in Congress prior to approval of the bill. Champ Clark, Speaker of the House, answered queries as to who had been responsible for founding of the Legion. He was asked specifically if Pershing was the one who called for Roosevelt's meeting, or was ordered to do so by the War Department. Clark replied that he was not certain, but continued that as far as he was able to tell it was "normal procedure" under the circumstances, since the soldiers had been restive and "had nothing to do." [44]

Before the Legion held its first convention on November 11, 1919, ex-Major Hamilton Fish, Jr., of New York, was delegated to write the Legion's preamble. It clearly stated the new Legion's concept of patriotism: "For God and for country we associate ourselves together for the following purposes: To uphold and defend the Constitution of the United States of America; to maintain law and order; to foster and perpetuate one hundred per cent Americanism; to preserve the memories and incidents of our association in the great war; to inculcate a sense of individual obligation to the community, state and nation; to make right the master of might; to promote peace and good will on earth; to safeguard and transmit to posterity the principles of justice, freedom and democracy; to consecrate and sanctify our comradeship by our devotion to mutual helpfulness." [45]

In comparison with the constitution and goals of the U.S.W.V. and the V.F.W., the Legion's contained some that was new and much that was old. It was generally a question of emphasis, but it showed a departure from the ideals of veteran brotherhood espoused twenty years previously. All of the conventional, traditional values of the earlier societies were enunciated: God, country, the Constitution, law and order, preservation of war memories, individualism, peace, good will, justice, freedom, democracy and fraternity. There was a change of pace in presentation, however; the U.S.W.V., and to a lesser extent, the V.F.W., put preservation of war memories and aid to needy comrades first, while the Legion put less emphasis on these goals in its preamble. The Legion identified God, the United States, and itself as being in concert and pledged itself to uphold the traditional cornerstones of the American heritage. The change of emphasis indicated that the always present moralism in official American societal pronouncements was more active than ever. The war was responsible. It helped nationally to institutionalize morality, God, and patriotism.

CHAPTER IV

CHRISTIAN KNIGHTS AND DISABLED VETERANS

A few days before he left the Presidency, Dwight D. Eisenhower made a significant valediction for a professional soldier who had thrown his political and social lot in with conservative business interests. He warned Americans that they must not allow a military-industrial axis to acquire too great power lest it gain dominance over our domestic and foreign affairs. The former president saw in his mind's eye a trend that appears to have been developing since the Munich Crisis of 1938. Today, almost by default, we are in a sense a semi-garrison state thanks to World War II and the Cold War. Major reliance upon diplomatic and economic measures against the Communists over the past years, rather than purely military moves, has made activists within the military and on the Far Right experience extreme frustration.

Currently people are aware that not only is there an industrial-military complex, but among some service personnel there exists a military-Radical Right nexus. So-called seminars jointly conducted by military officers and self-styled anti-Communist crusaders have sprung up across the country. Several of these rightist groups are Christian fundamentalist in a religious sense, and they effectively link the Cross and the flag in their crusades against all those with whom they disagree. The credentials of many of those who feel qualified to expound upon the dangers of Communism are highly suspect by other military men, scholars, diplomats, and assorted bureaucrats who have studied Communism under firm intellectual discipline and have appraised its work at first hand.

Numerous of the Christian patriots and their military cohorts infer that practically all domestic social reforms over the past thirty years have been the result of internal subversion conducted by devious Communist agents or their dupes. Such a Rightist military phenomenon is not new, for there was an analogous situation over a generation ago and, while a few of the ingredients that existed then are the same now, there is a major difference, too. The defense establishment was tiny at that time compared to what it is presently. However, the irritations engendered from being ignored or not having a particular set of programs enacted was endemic to the activists of yesterday just as of today. In the relatively more relaxed atmosphere of forty years ago, Americans tended to overlook and disregard soldiers whatever their ideologies were and no matter how sound or how unsound their views on any subject might be. Such an attitude of indifference infuriated a number of militarists who, in their own view, fought at God's hand and they tended to see something morally sinister and evil in a society that paid them so little heed. And, as events proved, in technical military affairs the nation ultimately was to pay a high price for not listening to much of what they said.

A generation ago, however, even among the veterans' groups who favored expanded military forces, there loomed larger issues. Most immediate was the need for medical facilities so that those who had suffered physical and mental wounds while on active service could be cared for decently. The doughboys of 1918, who were to extoll the virtues of national sacrifice and praise the merits of traditional American individualism, organized into blocs and looked to their government for medical and financial help. Meantime, a few among the more militaristic elements marched and countermarched in hurt pride and impatience.

*   *   *

Large and vigorous, the Legion could claim with some justification that it was democratic; its ranks, after all, were open to all veterans regardless of former rank. Another veterans' group appeared soon after the Legion but in contrast to the million-member society, the new organization was very exclusive indeed. It consisted only of officers.[1]

During World War I, some American liberals quixotically feared that when the military returned home thousands of officers might set up a para-military state. Although the War Department did not officially state such views, the professional officer corps possessed some equally quixotic conceptions about the American public.[2] With true lack of political imagination, the War Department set afoot a plan in 1919 whereby universal conscription was to continue after peace had been officially decreed. In the words of one critic commenting on the military mentality, it was "a golden moment" from the Army's viewpoint. Millions of war-trained men were available; war production had just hit its stride with the war's end; and during the war, the public generally seemed to have accepted the selective service system.[3]

From the office of the Chief of Staff came a pronouncement that if
America were invaded the people would have to field a trained army,
but that it could only be effective if backed by universal training
The public had trouble perceiving any threats from invaders and
the directive sank into a sea of silence. The "Great Reaction" to
the "Great Crusade" was in full swing as large segments of the public
turned away from the realities of world affairs. Many persons pin-
ned their hopes on a League of Nations; others thought that disarmament was the answer; a tremendous number returned to the concept
of isolationism; and practically all seemed to think that large armies
produced wars.[4]

The military establishment began to lose prestige and influence;
its views were often ignored and its pretentions were ridiculed. Critics
were unkind enough to point out that following the war West Point
operated with only half its classes filled. Thousands of regular officers
had resigned and thousands more non-commissioned officers had
deserted.[5] Although few persons expressed respect for servicemen,
not all officers appeared disenchanted with the military way. Some
of them wished to establish an organization of their own whose composition would be different than existing societies. A great many of
the comrades who were enrolled in the Legion and the Spanish-
American War groups came from the middle classes. Frequently, they
had become members because those organizations maintained auxiliary
groups. In terms of group behavior, the inclusion of females preserved
a family pattern. Despite societal ritual, there was an element of
folksiness in the joint gatherings of the older groups.[6]

But that type of sociability did not appeal to all former members
of the armed services. Many officers returned home to find that their
places of wartime pre-eminence had been taken by businessmen,
lawyers, doctors, and sometimes even by politicians! They also discovered that the new managerial society buffeted the olive drab patriot
about in an unseemly manner. The sacrifice, the dead comrades, the
fellowship, the caste prestige were too soon ignored by "the forgetful
mass."[7]

There was a note of restrained resentment on the part of some officers. In the words of one: "In the officers of the Great War we have
the elements that compose the greatest constructive force in the
America of today and in the America of the next thirty-five years.
They are men who brought trained intelligence and high spirit to the
task and many sacrificed greatly in undertaking it. They are men of
every creed and from every state, but the cross-section they form in

our national life is all that is best when we think of America and Americanism." [8]

Not enough Americans fully appreciated the role of officers in America. Something had to be done.

In the fall of 1920 a group of regular, reserve, and retired military officers met to form a protective association. They called themselves the American Officers of the Great War. The spirit and purpose of the group were outlined by a Major Almuth C. Vandiver. "By inheritance," said Major Vandiver, the officers that met in Detroit were the sixth generation of "the bald eagles (sic) brood of officers" who answered the Nation's call to arms. They, as officers, were uniquely qualified to help the country and this uniqueness he called, "qualification by descent." The officers assembled were not simply inheritors of the Revolutionary War's Order of the Society of the Cincinnati and the Civil War's Loyal Legion. They were in the proud tradition of the medieval Christian, Knights as well. The officers of the Great War were, in fact, contemporary Christian Knights.[9]

Vandiver spelled out the fears of the assembly and suggested counter-action. The group knew that a soldier's glory was ephemeral, but these officers were gathered to see that the fallen heroes had not died in vain. The men present were there to perpetuate the memories of the dead and "to impress ineradicably" upon the "inert and forgetful mass" of citizenry the "supremacy of their sacrifice." [10] The speech was a familiar one to the returned, insecure veterans seeking to relate the living members of society with the community of the dead. A pledge was taken to glorify the memories of the fallen. The deceased had been sacrificed in the crisis and were being used by the officers as an excuse to organize.[11] Nothing was new in this concept except the spirit in which it was accomplished. The officers were decidedly more militant than say, the U.S.W.V. They were bidden to "impress" such memories "ineradicably." They were "determined to be heard," and determined that "our influence be felt." [12]

Vandiver was elected Vice Commander-in-Chief of the new group. Its constitution pledged itself to refrain from engaging in politics or sectarian matters but it then blandly stated that one of its primary tasks, in addition to supporting the traditional pillars of the American heritage, was to help maintain a suitable military policy for the country. Presumably, the soldiers, who were determined to be heard, realized that this meant active interference in political affairs as military lobbyists.[13]

The newest veterans' society changed its name to The Military

Order of the World War (M.O.W.W.). It was a hereditary society,
open to all regular, reserve or retired commissioned personnel of the
military services and their sons. Its hierarchal structure was that of
a general staff. Furthermore, unlike the American Legion and the
V.F.W., its appeal was narrow and restricted. The M.O.W.W. was
not interested in mass support, although it was concerned with a
favorable impression within the community. Whereas the other
large veterans' organizations wanted community respect for a post and
the national organization, the M.O.W.W. asked for it as individual
leaders.[14]

Vice Commander Major Vandiver disjointedly and emotionally
explained the officers' obligations in a letter:

"Citizen officers of the American Expeditionary Force of the Army
of the United States.

HEARKEN!

"Impressed by the momentous showing by you at Armaged-
don the Congress of the United States has entrusted to you the important and responsible work of OFFICERING the Reserve Line of the
National Defense so long as you live. . . If the Eagle shrieked again
tomorrow you would be THERE even if you had to lie to the sympathetic
medico about your age and defective eyesight and overweight and flat
feet . . .

You KNOW the irresponsible, indomitable, superb and heroic YOUTH
OF AMERICA that all Hell can't stop would be THERE.

"Your boy and mine.

"And you KNOW, for you have been through the mill, that those
boys' elan and espirit and gay smiles in the teeth of red danger MUST
be tempered with CAUTION, AND COVER AND INDIVIDUAL INITIATIVE AND
THE TRICKS OF THE ENEMY so that the little white croses abroad and
the gold stars at home may be a little less numerous . . ."[15]

Speaking earlier to his officer comrades, Vandiver explained that
they possessed "common distinction," "common traditions," "common
responsibilities," and that they had served "no selfish ends. "We are
a great company . . . a great constructive force . . ." he wrote.[16] A
fellow officer echoed Vandiver. The M.O.WW. had a great mission,
said George A. Harris. As the logical descendant of the Order of
the Cincinnati, the M.O.W.W. was the only officer's society that
carried out the spirit of fight that the times demanded. Harris also
said that the M.O.W.W. was the only group capable of "guiding those
who cannot lead."[17] Lieutenant Colonel Charles W. Furlong seconded Vandiver and Harris in a letter to the National Headquarters. As

officers who lived within various American communities they constituted, Furlong contended, a potent influence that must be maintained.[18]

Americans seemed not to listen to the M.O.W.W. in its early days.
Apparently, those "unable to lead" were tired or apprehensive of those
able to do so. Not even all ex-officers felt beholden to the infant
society. The M.O.W.W. aimed at the goals of fostering the cultivation of military and naval service and working for the adoption of
a large military establishment, but Americans generally appeared
to regard militarism as something of an oddity.[19] Despite the fact
that the Armistice had been signed four years before, six M.O.W.W.
officers went in full uniform to Atlantic City in August, 1922 to set
up arrangements for the national convention. The sight of polished
leather and sparkling spurs was so unusual that the local press un-
believingly recorded their picture accompanied by a local politician
from the Jersey shore city.[20] As the months dragged on, National
Headquarters complained that there was no spirit of active co-operation in the recruitment of members for the Order. The society's *National Bulletin* reported: "the increase in membership has been
phenomically (*sic*) disproportionate to the amount and quality of
effort expended by the Chairman of the 'Committee on 100,000
members before 1930.' "[21]

In the Order's official eyes, another grave problem appeared during
the twenties—a wave of pacifism swept the country. If America became pacifistic, there were hard times ahead for a military order dedicated to the preservation of military forces and commemoration of
the war dead. Since such sentiment struck with devastating force at
the *raison d'etre* of the M.O.W.W., pacifists literally became dangerous
to the American inheritors of ancient knighthood.

With all the scorn and militancy of which they were capable, the
M.O.W.W. membership began to explode salvos against the new
enemy. Oswald Garrison Villard, editor of the liberal *Nation* magazine
was labeled "one of the most dangerous pacifists in the country." Villard was connected with subversive organizations, "one of the most
dangerous being the American Civil Liberties Union" (A.C.L.U.).
The A.C.L.U. actually "believes in rampant free speech," the *National
Bulletin* stated incredulously. Jane Addams, tireless, progressive reformer, was also singled out by the M.O.W.W. as a menace. Not even
the Christian churches were immune from such a dangerous doctrine, it
seemed. The Federal Council of Churches of Christ in America,
founded before the Great War as a part of the Protestant progressive
movement, was influenced by pacifists whose ideals the M.O.W.W.
found "questionable."[22]

The M.O.W.W. continued to strike at the insidiousness of pacifism,
but exposés and editorials were not enough and literature, too, was
wheeled into line. The soldier's poet, Rudyard Kipling, was drafted
for journalistic duty in a slightly modified form, to be sure, but he was
recognizable to the members. Kipling's ballad, "The 'Angin' of Danny
Deever," was rewritten and entitled "The Pacifists." The verses
ended:

> *'What's that so black agin the sun?,' said Files-on-Parade.*
> *'It's women fightin' hard for life,' the Color-Sergeant said.*
> *"What's that that whimpers overhead?,' said Files-on-Parade.*
> *'It's women's souls that's passin' now," the Color-Sergeant*
> *said.*
> *For they've broken up the Army, they had smashed it left*
> *and right,*
> *The Navy and the Air Force they'd abolish overnight,*
> *Made cowards of our young men, there was no one who would*
> *fight*
> *And an alien's took the country we were born in."*

The predilection for linking pacifism with femininity became something of a M.O.W.W. obsession during the twenties. In the spring of
1924, Jane Addams conducted a rally on behalf of the Women's International League for Peace and Freedom. The M.O.W.W. sent an
observer who reported back to the officers in disgust that he had noted
Bertrand Russell, "the effeminate, pacifistic representative of the
'Pink Intelligensia' of England," was there. Apparently, concluded
the witness, he was "the only male support of the ladies" in addition
to the "well-known pacifist" United States Senator, William E. Borah
of Idaho.[24]

Jane Addams, Bertrand Russell, and William Borah were not the
only prominent Americans honored by the M.O.W.W.'s attentions.
Felix Frankfurter and Zechariah Chafee, Jr. were scored as radical
and pacifistic. The Reverend Harry F. Ward and John Haynes Holmes,
both leaders of the newly organized A.C.L.U., were excoriated by the
officers for encouraging pacifist sentiments. Why, spluttered the
M.O.W.W.'s *Bulletin* editorially, the A.C.L.U. had even tried to infiltrate the services! Gloomily, it was pointed out that laws protected
such people and the nefarious doctrines that they preached, most of
which stemmed from the Sermon on the Mount. "We are entering
another dark age," the article concluded.[25] At one point, even the

professional heavyweight champion boxer of the world, Jack Dempsey, appeared pacifistic in the Order's eyes because of his failure to have seen war service.[26] The M.O.W.W. wanted to be fair, however, on the question of those anti-militarists who seemingly were busy undermining America. Some of the persons within the peace movements were honestly activated by a desire for peace, the *Bulletin* editorialized. These persons would, if the country were invaded, fight back but the remainder were beyond the pale. Most of these latter pacifists were "openly and avowedly international in their sympathies and opposed to nationalism . . . Internationalism and patriotism are antitheses; if one is an internationalist one cannot be called a patriot," the magazine reported.[27]

In true military fashion, the M.O.W.W. possessed plans and operations for dealing with the pacifist menace. The *National Bulletin* decided that "war time measures" were needed. "Oh, for a legislative Moses with a backbone and heart of steel who will get some law in effect that will stop these damnable activities," wailed the *Bulletin* with Old Testament intensity. Such legislation must be proper and just, said the *Bulletin*. On the other hand, it continued, the legislation would have to "wipe out" these disintegrating influences in government. Pacifism bordered on treason, and the M.O.W.W. was spiritually and constitutionally obliged "to crush treason." The choice of language employed by the society in its early days indicated not only its deep official feelings, but its reliance on force as an effective method of control in American society.[28]

At times it seemed to members of the M.O.W.W. that they fought a lonely battle. The Philadelphia Chapter heard Colonel John C. Groome, Eastern Penitentiary's warden, complain that he was not able to get anyone interested in the danger of pacifism. Such prominent conservatives as Charles Schwab and Judge Elbert H. Gary, head of the United States Steel Corporation, did not care. The "real enemies" of America are "those within," Groome continued. The M.O.W.W.'s great duty was to make the public aware of the dangerous threat of pacifism, the warden concluded.[29] Groome's talk stirred retired Major General Charles H. Muir to make a speech in which he came straight to the point: "I believe that it is our patriotic duty to find out who is putting money up for this dis-armament propaganda. We must rise against this creation of a race of cowards." [30]

The M.O.W.W. was especially alarmed about the activities of the National Committee for the Prevention of War, headed by Frederick J. Libby. The preachments of the organization were "insidious and destructive." Moreover, Libby was a slippery person because he "has brains and is therefore dangerous." [31]

Despite all its loud and thumping statements, the M.O.W.W.'s efforts during the twenties were generally ineffective. About the only people or groups that paid it any heed were those who were attacked by it, such as the A.C.L.U. Membership fell off; its scope and appeal were extremely limited as disarmament held obvious attractions for much of the country during that period. Even the Order admitted its ineffectiveness in regard to disarmament and pacifism; and its voice sounded harshly authoritarian and illiberal in its protests. The M.O.W.W.'s activities went unnoticed in the national press in contrast to the huge, boisterous American Legion. Despite its initial lack of publicity, the Order was to become more effective in the next two decades. As time progressed, the whole military establishment ceased to be a stepchild and inevitably grew up to head of the household as America neared World War II.[32]

In addition to the M.O.W.W., other more specialized veterans' organizations joined the growing ranks of patriotic groups founded since 1898. Two major veterans' societies created before the Second World War were the Disabled Veterans of America (D.A.V.), founded in 1920, and the Military Order of the Purple Heart (M.O.P.H.). The latter had been created by George Washington, forgotten for generations, and then resurrected in 1932. Membership in the last two groups depended upon wounds, injuries, or disabilities connected with military service.

Following the war the Legion had monopolized the issue of the disabled veterans. It charged that, in 1920, 15,000 men were hospitalized and that admissions ran to 2500 a month. The Legion also claimed that, from November 11, 1918 until late in 1920, no new hospitals had been built for war veterans. Half of the hospitalized men were in state, municipal, or private charity institutions. The Legion criticized the government because aid to the disabled was handled by three un-coordinated agencies. It further stated that the public had been led to believe by the Wilson administration that the disabled were cared for and rehabilitated.[33] The Legion pressed the fight and its spokesmen told of a dramatic scene that took place in Congress in December, 1919. Legionnaires brought wounded men from Walter Reed Hospital into the halls of Congress and confronted the lawmakers. According to reports, some Congressmen were seen to cry.[34]

The Legion had been a paramount promoter of aid to the disabled, but a feeling grew among the wounded that it took their own kind to understand their problems. In 1920 the Disabled Veterans of the World War formed an organization. The new group's function was "based on service" in the words of a National Commander. Its founder, Judge Robert S. Marx, from Cincinnati, Ohio, set up two headquarters. One remained in Cincinnati, but the legislative and rehabilitation divisions were located in Washington, D.C. The D.A.V. took slight issue with the Legion and claimed that it had been the first group to back creation of a Veterans' Bureau. The initial public response to the D.A.V. appeared heartening. The *Christian Science Monitor* reported that 1400 delegates attended the first convention and it recounted that Judge Marx wished the D.A.V. to inspire men to be self-supporting. Hearst's New York *American* carried a three column cartoon showing a one-legged doughboy covered with cobwebs waiting outside the doors of Congress.[35]

For a year, affairs went well for the D.A.V. and when the group met in San Francisco in 1922, they obtained much sentimental publicity. In more concrete terms, the D.A.V. drafted a legislative program for congressional action. The D.A.V. had the pleasure of seeing all the other veterans' organizations adopt virtually the same set of proposals. By 1924 the group had grown to include a "fun-making" organization within its ranks called "The Trench Rats." More important, it set up a co-ordinating body with both the V.F.W. and the American Legion.[36]

Bankruptcy and loss of membership plagued the D.A.V. from late 1924 until the boom times of 1928; meanwhile, it depended upon large grants extended by the Knights of Columbus. In 1925 the Knights informed the D.A.V. that its own treasury was depleted. The D.A.V. appeared to be disintegrating, headquarters announced. Despite economic ill-health and a definite lack of leadership, it pulled out of the red in 1928 and even increased its membership by one hundred chapters.[37] In the same year the Detroit Convention showed the country that the D.A.V. was vigorous. The lovable Trench Rats incited a riot that brought out the city's police and fire reserves. Socially it appeared that the D.A.V.'s conduct was not unlike the American Legion's.[38]

There were, however, differences. In some fields, such as national defense, immigration, and rehabilitation, the goals of both groups were often identical. In practice, however, the D.A.V. frequently acted differently from the Legion. It worked without regard to race, creed, or color among all the disabled. Unlike the Legion, it solicited help on behalf of the veteran without attempting to pressure him to join the

D.A.V. Perhaps the biggest difference, however, lay in public confessions of strengths and weaknesses. The Legion generally was well-heeled and possessed a large membership. The D.A.V., in the 1920's, was on just the opposite footing. Between 1920 and 1930, it publicly admitted that its membership vacillated between 25,000 to 35,000 persons while its potential membership was an estimated three quarters of a million. By 1930, the D.A.V. heard one of its own leaders state that "leadership has been lacking." No national Legion convention heard a similar remark made before its delegates.[39] There remained, however, the closest of co-operation between the two groups. Not only did some of their functions overlap as in the field of rehabilitation, but there was the question of dual membership. One D.A.V. National Commander estimated that ninety per cent of the D.A.V. membership belonged to the Legion and he also commented that the D.A.V. members were inclined to follow the Legion's lead in affairs not connected with veterans' issues.[40]

The Military Order of the Purple Heart was an organization akin to the D.A.V. The main concern of both societies was to provide services for the wounded or disabled veteran. The M.O.P.H., however, claimed an illustrous ancestry. The Purple Heart badge was created on February 7, 1782 by George Washington for enlisted personnel only. By contrast, in the same period, Washington's officers banded together in the Order of the Cincinnati. Except for the Cross of Saint George, awarded in the old Imperial Russian army, the Purple Heart remained the oldest decoration for valor in the Western World. When the British burned Washington, D.C. during the War of 1812, the Order's records were lost.[41]

In 1931 plans were made to commemorate Washington's two-hundredth birthday. President Herbert Hoover issued orders to the War Department to revive the organization. All World War I personnel who had been awarded Certificates of Merit or who had been wounded were to be given the decoration. On February 22, 1932, Chief of Staff of the United States Army, General Douglas MacArthur, sent out General Order Number Three reviving the M.O.P.H. out of respect to Washington's memory and military achievements.[42] The revival of the Order, however, attracted little attention. Only a few newspapers gave the event any coverage. The *New York Times,* which printed almost everything reported in connection with Washington's birthday, ignored the reactivation of the M.O.P.H.[43]

Lack of publicity plagued the organization all its subsequent career. The Order failed to gain members or influence despite the intensifica-

tion of the public's patriotism as America neared World War II. The
M.O.P.H. tried to capitalize on the upsurge of nationalistic sentiment.
For example, the formal manner of addressing a fellow member was to
call him "Patriot." Whereas, veterans in the other organizations
referred to each other as "Comrade." Despite such attempts to identify
the Order with growing national patriotism, few men joined the group.
By 1939, membership fell below fifteen hundred and the treasury yield-
ed a grand sum of $22.12. The voice of the M.O.P.H. was dimly heard,
if at all."

The three veterans' groups founded after the First World War were
as avowedly patriotic as their predecessors. They shared one other
aspect in common: all were restricted in appeal. The M.O.W.W.
was limited only to officers; the D.A.V. was open only to those who
suffered from physical or mental illness arising from war service; the
M.O.P.H. was limited to members of the Army who were either
wounded or awarded a Meritorious Conduct Certificate. Furthermore,
the latter was an organization directly revived and perpetuated by the
United States Army. None were well publicized principally because of
inadequate finances and restricted membership. Their net effect was
often negligible, save in the case of the D.A.V., whose rehabilitation
programs were often copied by the larger groups.

All of the veterans' societies, however, presented something more
than material benefits. They offered companionship and experiences
that could be shared without embarrassment. All seemed to conduct
themselves in a particular way and their patriotic activities led
critics to accuse them of excessive chauvinism. By their war service,
the veterans regarded themselves as special types of citizens. Under
such an interpretation, efficient platoon or small boat commanders
could pose as experts on all other matters. Patriotism became their
special privilege which they classified as Americanism. Often the
groups stated that Americanism was a principle, but in making such
a statement, the veterans did not explain that too often each individual
could read into a principle what he alone wished. Whether or not
Americanism was a principle or a symbol was to became a troublesome
point to the veterans' organizations.

CHAPTER V

WHAT IS 100 PER CENT AMERICANISM?

The veterans officially state that among other things Americanism is the spirit which has led the United States to victory in all its wars. Today almost everything appears to be either relative or of such complexity it defies simplification, and consequently there is a sense of tension and unease afoot as absolute standards and values become undermined by the impermanence of life. The meaning of Americanism has long been debated, and at this moment in our history the word and concept of victory also is under analysis by many members of the political community and ordinary citizens.

With the tasks confronting America, may the word victory be used in its conventional meaning? Yes, declare certain political leaders, several of whom are of extremely conservative persuasion. To them and numerous other Americans the Cold War is a forty-year-old battle defined simply as Americanism versus Communism and which may be won by preserving traditional ideals through policies of non-aid to any neutralist countries dealing with the Communists, using the United Nations only when it suits our foreign policy, expanding our military forces, cutting taxes, and decentralizing the Federal government at home. The critics of this approach state that the fundamental problems facing us could not possibly be met by such contradictory and unsophisticated means. They point out that an enlarged military could hardly be supported by cutting taxes, nor does it suggest a non-concentration of power and that, while modernized military forces are needed for deterrence, they must not expand too greatly for they then could come to dominate domestic and foreign policies. Furthermore, because the nature of Communism itself alters over periods of time, new techniques are called for to suit changing situations; finally, the United Nations is not ours to unilaterally utilize, since neutralists, Communists, and our own coalition of power all balance each other and we must live together or perish. But the dispute will continue as it has done in the past, for words and their meanings change from century to century and from one era to the next.

Thus the nineteenth century's liberal is today's conservative; in 1906 a progressive was a civic-minded reformer, but among Americans cap-

tured by the Communists in Korea it came to mean those who col-
laborated with the enemy. Over forty years ago such terms as Americanism and victory held a definite image for Theodore Roosevelt and
his age, and he passed these beliefs onto his sons and their generation
who joined various of the veterans' associations. Since then they have
never doubted in their basic concept of victory, but almost at once
upon organizing they struggled and have continued to do so with a
definition of Americanism as they tried to impose its image upon a
pluralistic society.

* * *

Of all the veteran's organizations founded since 1898 the American
Legion was the first to use officially the phrase 100 per cent Americanism. It appeared in the preamble of the Legion's Constitution, but
not in the first draft of that document. At the St. Louis caucus in
May, 1919, a subcommittee wrote the preamble after an all-night
session. Finally, it was submitted to a committee where, "at the last
moment," the percentage figure was added before the word Americanism. The phrase then read "to foster and perpetuate 100 per cent
Americanism." [1]

The language was vigorous, but it did not define Americanism *per
se*. Almost at once, the Legion was constrained to explain the term
and it retained Ivy Lee, pioneer public relations expert, to analyze the
phrase. Lee admitted there would be considerable discussion on what
was or was not 100 per cent Americanism. He stated that because
of the members' war records the Legion was imbued with 100 per
cent Americanism and that it was opposed to "Bolshevism, anarchy
and disorder." The article stated what 100 per cent Americanism was
not; the question of the words' real meaning remained unanswered. [2]

The term had come from the father of the Legion's primary founder.
Theodore Roosevelt, Jr., according to the Legion, picked the phrase
up from the former president while the latter campaigned for American
preparedness prior to World War I. [3] The elder Roosevelt had kept
many ideals in mind while he enunciated his views on Americanism.
As early as 1894, he declared that Americanism "was a question of
spirit, conviction, and purpose" while it was not a question of creed or
birthplace. [4] But his views began to shift after World War I broke
out, and shortly before the United States entered the war he wrote to
S. Stanwood Menken, president of the National Security League,
that the attributes of Americanism were unquestioned loyalty to the

flag, free education, equal rights, freedom of speech, genuine representative government, and genuine political and religious freedom. Also
included by the former President were "the virtues of courage, justice,
truth, sincerity, and hardihood—the virtues that made America." [5]
Roosevelt's ideals appeared to be conventional, but he added a few
interpretations peculiar to his own philosophy. All that was un-
American, Roosevelt said, included those things in American society
which led to "either government by plutocracy or government by
mob." What America had to fear was "prosperity-at-any-price,"
"peace-at-any-price," and "the love of soft living." [6]

Co-equal in Roosevelt's mind with the traditional virtues of Americanism was a problem born out of the new immigration and high-
lighted by war-time tensions involving the "hyphenated American"
who, although he lived in the United States, felt an emotional pull
toward the country of his birth. Roosevelt deeply and emotionally
feared, as did many Americans, that the hyphenate held a dangerously
dual allegiance. "The hyphen," said Roosevelt, "is incompatible with
patriotism." [7]

The question of the hyphenated Americans was heavily underlined
when the United States entered the war in 1917 because the hyphenates posed a difficult problem in regard to the nation's security. It
was hard to determine how much of a threat they constituted to the
war effort. Under patriotic stimulus or its guise, persons called attention to the issue of dual allegiances and leaders as well as individuals
raised a single standard by which to measure Americanism. When
a nation decides that its national existence might be imperiled, it
frequently curtails traditional liberties in the national interest, as Lincoln's administration had done during the Civil War. The hyper-
excited conduct of American leaders and the public has to be seen
within the emotional context of World War I to understand the treatment accorded the hyphenates. As a greatly beloved leader, Roosevelt's sense of duty compelled him to express his deep concern to the
public and this feeling combined with his earlier uneasiness over unrestricted immigration. The fusion resulted in Roosevelt's wartime
version of Americanism which was eagerly embraced by many persons
and has continued to remain the only acceptable model to some in
their distress over an America internally in flux and menaced by unfriendly foreign powers. Roosevelt said that he desired to buttress
America's security above all else, and in the early spring of 1918 he
told the country that there could be no such thing as a fifty-fifty

allegiance. His voice and words were heard and read by respectful millions in the months before his death.[8]

The complex issue of the hyphenates did not die when the war ended. The American postwar period became marked by hysteria which had been generated by war passions. Some citizens engaged in acts of violence and many talked the language of force. The veterans' organizations naturally were not immune to this emotionalism. Caught in the aftermath of this hysteria, the ex-servicemen found new dangers as bolshevists, foreigners, and pacifists became their special targets. The Legion faced these problems at once during the first national convention, held in Minneapolis on November 11, 1919. The Legionnaires called for the establishment of an Americanism Commission whose purpose was the realization of 100 per cent Americanism by means of a comprehensive program. It took five years for the program to appear, but in the meantime, the Legion tried to attain 100 per cent Americanism by direct means and legislative action.[9]

In the summer and late fall of 1919, the hyphenate helped the Legion in its efforts to determine Americanism. The hyphen, in this case, was the alien who had refused to serve in the armed forces during the war. Understandably perhaps, the Legion referred to these persons as alien slackers. Posts and individual Legionnaires petitioned Congress to deport them. Using the slacker as a negative symbol of un-Americanism, and the ex-serviceman as a positive symbol of Americanism, the Legion pushed a vigorous drive to have the aliens deported. The Legion's official magazine, the *American Legion Weekly*, under the editorship of Colonel George White and Harold Ross, sounded the opening note of the campaign against the slackers.[10]

Charles D. Kelley wrote in the *Weekly* that the veterans understood and personified Americanism because they had fought for it but by contrast, the alien slacker had ducked his obligation to the country of his residence by refusing to serve. Kelley contended that by such a refusal the alien proved himself to be un-American. Kelley then called upon his readers to demand that the Federal Government publish the names of all alien slackers and conscientious objectors. If the names were published, public opinion would force the slackers and objectors to feel uncomfortable in the glare of publicity. Kelley concluded that the pressure of this opinion would force the slacker to leave the country.[11] In 1921, the War Department released the names of all alien slackers in its files and the *Congressional Record* printed them. This marked the apex of the alien slacker campaign. Although the Legion failed to achieve an exact definition of 100 per cent Americanism during the drive, the alien slacker served as a useful example of un-Americanism to it.[12]

Another symbol of un-Americanism speedily replaced the alien slacker. The Legion's dislike of the alien was transferred to the Marxist. In combatting Marxism's various forms, the veterans' organization adopted the attitude that any situation of which the Legion disapproved could be labeled as Communist.[13] In 1919, during a Denver street car strike, the local Legion post policed the downtown area and, in a few cases, tried to break picket lines. The *Weekly* commended the Legionnaires for their spirit of Americanism in attempting to curb un-American labor radicalism. The magazine, however, refused to sanction the destruction of a small amount of property by Legionnaire "policemen" saying "it can only lead to bad publicity for the National Organization . . ."[14]

The bad publicity arising from certain illegal acts by Legionnaires hurried plans for the proposed Americanism Commission at the National Headquarters. One of the first problems faced by the embryonic Commission was the question of 100 per cent Americanism. The *Weekly* told its readers that the new group had tackled the issue immediately. The magazine stressed the fact that rather than trying to work out a pat definition, the Commission would attempt to conduct "a program which in its final approved form will be a detailed definition of what is meant by '100 per cent Americanism' . . ."[15]

The Legion admitted that, lacking a working definition of the phrase, it frequently found itself embarrassed by Americanization work which did not always jibe with its constitution.[16] As if to heighten the embarrassment, Legionnaires continued acts which violated the Legion's pledge of maintaining law and order. In Carpenteria, California, local Legionnaires whipped a newspaper editor with whom they were not in sympathy; and in March, 1921, a group of Legionnaires attempted to stop a Farmers Non-Partisan League meeting at Great Bend, Kansas, by beating up four men driving to the assembly.[17] The newly born American Civil Liberties Union reported in 1921 that, since its founding, the Legion had been guilty of engaging in no less than fifty illegal acts of violence.[18] Criticism from within and without the Legion welled up and the acts of violence dropped off appreciably as a result of the publicity.[19] The National Headquarters took note of the A.C.L.U.'s criticism and adopted a policy it has supported over a forty year period. Since 1921 the Legion annually has demanded that the A.C.L.U. be investigated by the Attorney General's office as an un-American organization.[20]

The first chairman of the Americanism Commission, Arthur Woods, former police commissioner of New York, announced in 1920 that a definition of 100 per cent Americanism might soon appear and that it would be neither narrow nor reactionary.[21] After a year's work, the Commission's program failed to materialize, but a definition of Americanism was presented. Franklin D'Olier, first National Commander, stated on behalf of the Commission that "100 per cent Americanism is fair play for all those who play fair." In the same year National Headquarters announced that a workable definition should accompany the program when it appeared. This reversed the earlier decision that the program itself should represent the definition.[22]

Not until 1923 was another definition available. This one read: "Americanism is nationalism and patriotism. It is that spirit which has led us to victory in all our wars." The concept was vague and martial in tone. The Legion was getting close to an official definition but it still nibbled at the periphery.[23] In 1924, the Americanism Commission officially went into full operation. By 1925, the Director of the Commission, Garland Powell, wrote a handbook on Americanism that contained the definition as first stated in 1923. No record has been found showing the public's reaction to such a militant appraisal. The Legion wanted an enlarged military establishment, but Congress had not voted for military expansion and during those years many Americans were disenchanted with the martial spirit.[24]

Other veterans' organizations as well as the Legion wrestled with the Americanism problem during the early twenties. The M.O.W.W.'s position on Americanism had been stated by Captain Sherrad Ewing in 1921.[25] Other M.O.W.W. officers embraced a more Rooseveltian view, stating that the principles of liberty, justice, hard work, and clean living were identical with Americanism. One colonel in particular wrote in 1922 that foreign propagandists and groups were trying to organize against the principles of Americanism. "Never," said the colonel, "has there been a greater need for a clear-cut idea of what our country is to stand for and for an uncompromising Americanism on the part of every loyal citizen than now." The tiny M O.W.W. needed assistance, however, the officer said; he recommended that the Order join its far less exclusive brother organization, the Legion, to help put "none but Americans on guard."[26]

While the M.O.W.W.'s patriotism depended on a caste system, the Legion's patriotic appeal was pegged at the former enlisted man's level of humor and interest. Such appeals were materialistic or activist taking the form of community projects or slacker

drives.[27] The M.O.W.W. wanted action, too, but it wished to direct
the shock troops of Americanism. The Order boasted that no group
was more potent, or had greater influence in maintaining the status
of Americanism. Another member commented that if the Legion and
the Order co-operated, they could be "the bulwark" of Americanism
within the country.[28]

During the early twenties not all Americans, however, regarded
Americanism as viewed by the veterans' organizations and other
groups as a force for good. A writer for the *North American Review* in
1922 said that Americanism veered off into "exhibitions of reckless
independence" in both domestic and foreign affairs. "True Americanism," wrote Lindsey Blayney, " (is) a spirit of co-operation for the
common good." [29] F. B. Kaye echoed Blayney's views in an article in
the liberal periodical, *The Nation*, in the summer of the same year.
Americanism as practiced in the early twenties, Kaye alleged, was
intolerant provincialism. The veterans' groups were not the worst
practitioners, he said, for the twenties saw a mass revival of the Ku
Klux Klan that also acted in the name of Americanism. The schools,
Kaye decided, suffered the worst from patriotic societies and the Klan.
Patriotism and Americanism were, he thought, basic to most students
in the form of loyalty, whether it was to the gang or devotion to national heroes; Americanism need not be aroused, it had to be directed
by a liberal and critical education. "Ultimate patriotism," Kaye concluded, "should be based, not on flagwaving, but on knowledge and
tolerance." [30]

Little change, however, took place in the veterans' approach to
Americanism during the mid-twenties. Such work within the V.F.W.
and the Legion from 1924 until 1927 entailed little that was dramatic.
The V.F.W. was chronically hampered by a lack of funds, and the
Legion concentrated on revising its Americanism administrative machinery. The emphasis on Americanism increasingly shifted to material programs rather than analyzation. There appeared to be a lack
of cohesiveness and direction about the desirable aims of Americanism
expressed by the largest veterans' groups despite much militant talk.
Such vagaries apparently were common to all the societies for, as the
twenties neared mid-point, the U.S.W.V.'s spokesmen revealed a
continuing sense of uneasiness about American society.

In 1924 a member made an assessment of America for the delegates
to the national encampment. Americanism, the members heard, was
love of country but there were "elements of decay" within the nation.
Deaths due to industrial accidents, divorces, the great number of

illiterate voters, speed, and mob violence, were dangers that needed to be watched.[31] Comrade Winfield Scott, Commissioner of Pensions for the Veterans Bureau, tried to reassure the insecure U.S.W.V. in 1926 at the Des Moines National Encampment. Scott sized up his audience—overwhelmingly middleaged—and defined progressive Americanism for the U.S.W.V. as the need for the protection of the aged and the young, the infants and dependent ones. The aged had to be protected, he continued, because of the good they had done the country during their lifetime. The infants needed protection for they were the future citizens and they had to have the right principles of government instilled into their young hearts.[32] In 1927 the U.S.W.V.'s Patriotic Instructor described Americanism in terms that were typical of the group's thoughts and feelings on the subject:

The four-square people, solid through and through,
The land secure, to traditions true;
That people and that nation must depend,
Upon quadruple strength unto the end.

Upon the purity of home, and then
Intelligence of all its coming men;
Upon religion, liberty secure,
And love of law that ever shall endure.

The home, the school, the church, and under all,
The Constitution, these must never fall;
These are the pillars of our temple fair,
Preserve, support them, you, who love—and dare! [33]

In a speech before the Baltimore convention in 1927 the Commander-in-Chief of the M.O.W.W. for that year, Douglas MacArthur, noted that the group's efforts were stymied by its small numbers. The M.O.W.W. had failed to expand and its sentiments and ideals were not attracting a large membership, MacArthur pointed out, because of duplication of effort among the veterans' societies. The officers of all the wars should, he felt, be in one group, corresponding largely to the American Legion. The goals of Americanism, as the M.O.W.W. saw them, were endangered by the fragmentation of effort among so many societies. "Everywhere," MacArthur concluded, "practical men realize that in the complexity of modern life strength, no less than economy, comes from unity." [34]

Toward the end of the 1920's a major breakthrough occurred for all the veterans except the M.O.W.W. in regard to the troublesome question of Americanism. Senator Rice Means, Colorado, Republican, former National Commander of the V.F.W. (1914-1915) and Commander-in-Chief of the U.S.W.V., called for a private conference on national defense. Attending the meeting, held in Means' office at the Capitol on February 18, 1927, were James Tanner, Past National Commander of the G.A.R.; Howard P. Savage, National Commander of the American Legion; Theodore Stitt, Commander-in-Chief of the V.F.W.; and John V. Clinnin, National Commander of the D.A.V.[35] The main purpose of the meeting was to endorse a national defense program. This was accomplished, but also as a result of this gathering, the five veterans' organizations agreed on a definition of Americanism: "Americanism is an unfailing love of country; loyalty to its institutions and ideals; eagerness to defend it against all enemies; undivided allegiance to the flag and a desire to secure the blessings of liberty to ourselves and posterity." [36]

The Legion heavily embroidered this statement in the years that followed, but it has never claimed to have created the definition despite its prior years of effort to do so. The U.S.W.V. incorporated the paragraph into its ritual, and every camp (post) meeting and every session of a National Encampment begins with all the comrades standing and repeating the code in unison. This observance has been followed religiously by them since 1927. Although the Legion and other groups use the definition, it is not necessarily a regular part of their ritual.[37]

The definition of 100 per cent Americanism was officially solved by most veterans' societies in the twenties, although they continued to elaborate on and worry about it in later years, but many Americans outside the patriotic groups were as perplexed as the ex-servicemen. In roughly the same period the magazine, *Forum*, announced the results of a contest it had held for the purpose of defining Americanism. The journal reported that it received a tremendous variation of themes that ranged from George Washington to the baseball player-turned-evangelist, Billy Sunday. One contributor suggested that Americanism was "the national inferiority complex." [38]

Two years after Means' meeting, the stock market crashed, America entered the Great Depression and with the rest of the nation the veterans' societies suffered. The National Patriotic Instructor of the V.F.W. reported in 1932 that Americanism activities had been curtailed because of the depression. Money for the Instructor's work had been located in a New York bank which closed its doors in 1931. Americanism had meant Americanization of the immigrant to the V.F.W. in the twenties and during the depression, supported by the other veterans' organizations, it wanted all immigration stopped. As in the case of the Legion, a few of the veteran societies maintained Americanization programs that were integral parts of their Americanism plans. The V.F.W. voiced the sentiments of all in saying that the polygot American population needed but "one flag, one language, and one homogeneous race," but there was certainly no explanation as to whether or not the statement was an official endorsement of racial amalgamation.[39]

The M.O.W.W. echoed the V.F.W. almost to the syllable. Economic conditions were so bad by 1931 that the organization cancelled its annual convention. Membership of the Order fell below 3,500, of whom only 2,700 were fully paid. Americanism, to the M.O.W.W. in that desperate year, was symbolized by the slogan "America for Americans." To make sure that this type of Americanism was perpetuated, the M.O.W.W. urged restrictive immigration and deportation of all aliens who were in the country illegally.[40] By 1932 the M.O.W.W. again was able to hold its annual convention and it regained some of its old fire. The primary speaker was the colorful and outspoken Deputy Chief of Staff of the United States Army, Major General Van Horn Mosely who later became a leader of a Radical Right movement investigated by Congress. He told an enthusiastic audience that the M.O.W.W. represented "the cream of all our veteran organizations." Thanks to the M.O.W.W.'s co-operation, the Regular Army was in better shape than ever before, Mosely disclosed. No one understood the precepts of real Americanism as well as military officers. "The khaki," he continued, "has simply taken the place of the armor of old"; officers today are "Christian Knights, just as we are the Christian Army of a Christian nation." Moreover, he revealed, the M.O.W.W. marched better to the tune of "Onward Christian Soldiers" than any other song; the mission of the Order was clear. The military services, in short, were needed more than ever to guarantee the future of America. As Mosely stepped back from the rostrum he dramatically cried: "Peace, peace, there is no peace," and, as the Old Testament wail echoed throughout the hall, the M.O.W.W. delegates rose up and vigorously applauded.[41]

Under the impact of the depression years fissures other than economic split the social and psychological mosaic of America. Bewildered and frustrated citizens listened to all types of persons and newly formed organizations that offered solutions or remedies for the ills of the country. The veterans were organized better than most to capitalize on this state of unsettledness for they had long felt that the United States was being undermined by a sinister conspiracy of forces that gnawed away at the nation's core of Americanism. The complexity of the society and the malaise brought about by the depression seemed only to emphasize the desperate fragmentation of the national soul. Plainly, to the veterans, what was needed was a tightening of the standards of nationalism. There had to be a return to basic Americanism. Of the major veterans' societies, the Legion was in the most advantageous position to direct this particular fight due to its size and wealth.

As if to symbolize the problem at hand and indicate the course of direction, by 1936 the Legion was hearing a new voice defining Americanism. It belonged to Homer Chaillaux, a veteran and erstwhile Los Angeles postman who had been appointed to the Americanism Commission of the Legion in 1935. By the next year he became its full-time paid director, a post he occupied until his death in 1945. During his reign no man used the phrase 100 per cent Americanism more assiduously and no man spoke on the subject of Americanism with more certainty than he. Regardless of what the individual Legionnaire might have thought on the subject, it was Chaillaux's interpretations that the National Headquarters in Indianapolis proclaimed and it was his pronouncements that bore the Legion's full official weight.[42]

Chaillaux, as had many Legionnaires before and have many since, found the easiest method of explaining 100 per cent Americanism was to list attitudes or ideals thought to be un-American. Consequently, his views on Americanism were often stridently negative rather than positive. In 1936 he set the tone for his directorship of the National Americanism Commission in a book entitled, *Isms,* which, among other things, excoriated the Communist Party of the United States and deplored the rise in membership of fascist organizations throughout America. The author employed the terms "100 per cent Americanism" and "un-American" throughout the book and persons and groups whom he branded as un-American included: the A.C.L.U.; Socialist, Norman Thomas; Nazi Bundist, Fritz Khun; Professor Felix Frankfurther of the Harvard Law School; and Methodist Bishop Francis J. McConnell, head of the Federal Council of Churches of Christ in America.[43]

Chaillaux even proceeded to find evidence of un-Americanism within the Legion itself. In 1936 the Americanism Committee of the New York County, New York Department, printed its own pamphlet entitled, "Americanism: What Is It?" written by C. LeRoy Baldridge, a writer, artist, and Legionnaire. The pamphlet was, in Baldridge's words "a simple restatement of the familiar principles of American ideology." Civil liberties and an emphasis on humanistic relations with the world at large were the main themes. The pamphlet was a great success within New York and requests for reprints arrived written on "the embossed pages of Wall Street" as well as on "grimy postcards in broken English." [44] The New York County Americanism Commission was surprised but pleased at the reception. The pamphlet was, after all, an elementary declaration of American idealism. When Chaillaux examined the booklet, however, he angrily called it "an illegitimate Legion offspring" and charged that Baldridge had placed much too much emphasis on freedom of speech and not enough on the fundamentals of religion. His sense of Americanism was further outraged by the fact that the book's paper was Japanese and, furthermore, the American eagle on the cover was printed in red. All of these criticisms were weighted with significance to Chaillaux whose final objection was Baldridge's contention that American welfare depended upon others in the world community. [45] Under pressure by the State and National Headquarters, the New York County Americanism Committee hurriedly withdrew the pamphlet. Liberals protested the headquarter's interference and *The New Republic* editorially likened the Legion's action to an approval of fascism. [46]

Baldridge confidently announced that the matter would be brought before the autumn National Convention where there would be a discussion on Americanism and its definition. Then, said Baldridge, the whole Legion would declare itself in favor of the Bill of Rights, the Constitution, and the Declaration of Independence. The convention, the embattled author stated, would reveal a new sense of liberalism or else it would display a body of former patriots in the grip of reactionary leadership, ripe for demagogs. [47] The latter was the closest to the truth. There was no new definition of Americanism at the Convention, and Baldridge and his supporters were cautioned not to deviate from National Headquarter's policy. National Commander Ray Murphy praised Homer L. Chaillaux for his devotion. The National Americanism Chairman, Stephen F. Chadwick, told the assembled delegates that the Commission was mindful that there were some Legionnaires unacquainted with the National program and in their ignorance they had criticized without comprehending the program's magnitude. He urged such critics to make a careful study before they deprecated the program. Chadwick ended with the observation that the Commission's work had been received with overwhelming support.[48]

The New Republic's charge, however, that the Legion had endorsed a form of fascism was too harsh. The Legion was a gigantic corporation with close to two million members located in every state and territory of the union. In any group of such size, power tends to gravitate to a small minority. Without such a small clique in control, the bulky membership would display even less cohesion than it does. Research shows that membership on key committees within a vast structure naturally fall to those who have the leisure time for such activities and it becomes almost impossible to remove such persons once in office. An officer in such a position of importance cannot help but become isolated in the performance of duty. Having developed a special skill, as in Chaillaux's case, the expert becomes indispensable.[49] The rank and file of the Legion or most of the societies are preoccupied with everyday affairs and the organization's primary importance lies in their social lives. The average member is in no sense a professional veteran. In contrast, Chaillaux was a professional veteran at the National Headquarters where he lived a bureaucratically isolated life.[50]

Chaillaux's beliefs of what constituted 100 per cent Americanism might be questioned but his actions and the support he always received from the Legion hierarchy cannot be construed to mean that all Legionnaires automatically sanctioned everything he said or did. Later, during the Second World War and several times following the war, the top echelons of the Legion stated views and policies that ran counter to the desires of the Legion as a whole. The result in all cases was an unfavorable reaction on the part of the rank and file. Publicity conscious to a fault, the Legion always has tried to minimize such revolts and keep them out of the press. The American Legion, however, is hardly unique in this respect. As one student of pressure groups has demonstrated amply, the labor unions, the National Association of Manufacturers, and the American Medical Association, to name but three types of organizations, have all fallen heir to the same practices and mistakes of the Legion. The Chaillaux-Baldridge incident of 1936 signified a degree of internal stress within the Legion, but precisely how much dissension it symbolized was difficult to assess. The furor over the Americanism pamphlet died down after the national convention and the incident was never officially referred to again.[51]

The Legion, meanwhile, like other veterans' societies, turned from internal problems to international affairs. Increasingly, from 1936 to 1939, the veterans' organizations became preoccupied with events

across the seas. In this regard, the groups mirrored the concern of
the public and by 1939 the nation's mood was complex as citizens
began to consider the merits and demerits of isolation from world
problems. Controversy and interest over the depression and domestic
reform subsided under the press of European and Asian affairs.[53]

As the world teetered, veered and finally entered World War II the
Legion's and V.F.W.'s conventions met annually and officially thrashed
out the problems connected with America's involvement. Like the
general public, the veterans were hotly split on the isolationist issue,
but unmistakenly world events dominated the two largest assemblies.
The isolationists tended to make their views prevail with the result
that the two major societies officially echoed many sentiments of the
America First organization. In truth, isolationism had obviously long
been a dominant factor in the veterans' Americanism ideology. Great
emotionalism was engendered by the 1939-1941 controversy but all it
really did was to emphasize long-held beliefs of the major organizations' hierarchy. A cardinal tenet of such Americanism was that the
nation should, indeed, remain apart from the Old World's
affairs and let Europe stew in her own rotten juices. At the same time,
however, the United States must arm to the teeth, intensify nationalism at home by concerted patriotic campaigns, and purify the country by ridding it of all that was subversive or un-American. Sadly, as
all too many know, subversives and un-Americans traditionally included not only suspected fascists and communists, but those who
held non-conformist views. Civil liberties took repeated beatings at
the hands of convention committees.

Not until the Battle of Britain was well under way and not until
major British cities were being smashed by the *Lufwaffe* did the
Legion's high command reverse its isolationist stand. And then it was
done in a spirit that American aid was but an extension of American
security. There were few official gestures on the part of any of the
veterans' societies in cognizance of the fact that for one awful year
the British Empire alone resisted tyranny for the free societies of the
world. Although as individuals many organized veterans held inter-
ventionist beliefs, they did not find official expression. Not even the
M.O.P.H., men who knew better than most other veterans the anguish
of personal suffering, were officially prepared to support the British by
all aid short of war. It is possible that their very suffering made them
reject the idea of combat, but their expressions of Americanism
during the period are narrowly militant, and vaguely generalized.
Concerned as the Purple Hearters were with the war, they were just

as preoccupied with their small numbers and general lack of publicity and power.[53]

Although World War II affected most of the societies, it seemed to pass by the U.S.W.V. Following the war's outbreak, it was unable to equate its concept of Americanism with life in the war forties. A new generation had appeared, Junior Vice Commander-in-Chief Joe R. Hanley plaintively announced in 1940, which had been born in soft times and had forgotten "the Boys of ninety-eight." The "boys," furthermore, were dropping off rapidly at the rate of six thousand in one year. The men who fought in the Spanish-American War had represented Americanism by their sacrifices. The comrade's deeds had been unfairly belittled, Hanley charged, for the war in 1898 had not been easy. That war had not cost the Government a cent, he added somewhat inaccurately, but its participants were the ones who had paid.[54] Hanley restated the theme of Americanism as the U.S.W.V. typically saw it on the eve of America's entry into history's bloodiest conflict:

"I am not an emotional man . . . but I was stirred when I heard the chorus of Americanism . . . We are determined that the ideals of our dead shall be the ideals of our Nation . . . Our comrades saluted the flag . . . for its red stripes of sacrifice. The color made fast in the shed blood of thousands of our strongest, best, virile manhood . . . We salute the white stripe of purity, washed clean with the tears of the wives and mothers and daughters who stayed behind and mourned those who never came back. We salute it for the blue field of constancy that has never wavered in its idea of freedom, and we salute it for the twinkling star of hope that even in this dark hour shines out to all the world undimmed in its luster and its glory.[55]

Chaplain-in-Chief Fred R. Hamilton manifestly spoke for the delegates when he told Hanley, "It has been very difficult for us to refrain from loud amens and applause . . . May God bless this message . . ." The comrades then stood and sang "God Bless America." [56]

The Disabled Veterans of America met in the same year and also considered the Americanism problem but more within the context of the times than the U.S.W.V. The war intensified the search for the key to Americanism as nationalism popularly manifested itself in a surge of patriotic spirit. The D.A.V. came up with the most expeditious analysis of all the veterans' groups to that date. The society, despite having agreed to the 1926 joint definition, was not pleased with it in the years that followed. A special committee was appointed to make a study and finally, after a careful inquiry, it reported that there were so many definitions of Americanism that it would take volumes to set them all down in print. The Committee decided, accordingly, that Americanism was best defined by the Constitution, the various state constitutions, and the Bill of Rights. That being the case, the committee said, "a detailed definition was unnecessary to the convention." [57] What the D.A.V. needed, the group reported, was a practical expression of Americanism which meant a community-level program that embraced patriotic education and service to distressed comrades. But the report also avowed that there was no place in America for anyone not in direct and complete accord with the principles of the American Government. Dissenting opinion was not popular with the D.A.V. and, under the impetus of the rising martial spirit, the organization stated that there was no room in America for anyone who was not willing to make extensive sacrifices. Education, service, sacrifice, National Defense, and belief in the tenets of democracy made up the elements of 100 per cent Americanism and the entire concept depended upon a belief in God. [58]

In 1944 the leaders of the Order of the Purple Heart tried their hands at analyzing the abstraction. The concept actually was a question of Americanization rather than simple Americanism, Patriot Henry C. Fuller, Sr. wrote to members of the M.O.P.H. in 1944: "Patriots of the Purple Heart—battle-tested in all branches of our armed forces, who better than *we* are entitled to 'Americanize Americans'—We, who have been 'blood-donors' to supply blood plasma to restore the 'red' in the 'Red—White—and Blue' as true red-blooded Americans, appreciating full well, our rights and privileges as citizens of the greatest Nation on the face of the globe! Patriots—we can—we must—we will 'Americanize Americans', aiding in every way humanly possible, our armed forces to win this World War II!" [59]

Patriot Fuller's words failed to spell out precisely what he meant by "Americanization of Americans." As usual, there was an intimation that the M.O.P.H. had set an example for Americans by having been wounded.

A month after the United States dropped its first atomic bomb on Japan which introduced a whole new concept of world survival, the U.S.W.V. met in Denver. The convention expressed its gratitude that the war had been won. Speakers talked of McKinley, who was likened to "Peter the Hermit bearing the Holy Cross," and the depravities of "the cruel ravaging Spaniards." Chaplain-in-Chief James M. Todd brought applause from the delegates when he stated that patriotism abided only as long as the public showed gratitude for loyal service to country. The Spanish-American War had shown that one generation

of Americans lived Americanism by fighting for their ideal of freedom
and liberty for an oppressed people. That war also had settled great
issues unlike the others which followed it, the chaplain continued.
"Never again has haughty, imperious Spain dared to impose her
tyrannies upon any people in the Western Hemisphere," he reminded
his audience.[60]

The V.F.W. had dwindled to 250,000 members on the eve of World
War II. For reasons that were not entirely clear even to the V.F.W.,
the membership shot up to over a million members following the war.
With the increase in numbers came more money and a larger organizational structure. The Americanism Committee of the V.F.W.
expanded its activities and, in 1951, announced its meaning of 100 per
cent Americanism. It meant active, positive patriotic defense of the
country during peace and war to create security, Mark Kinsey, Americanism Director, told the delegates to the fifty-second National Encampment. "Neighborliness" created unity, Kinsey said, and in unity
there was security. Conceivably, real 100 per cent Americanism was
a cultivation of neighborliness and that was the only way in which the
V.F.W. knew how to carry on its Americanism work.[61] By 1954 the
V.F.W. gave up using any pat definition of 100 per cent Americanism.
Kinsey announced to a National Encampment held in Philadelphia
that Americanism in the future meant all details pertaining to the
development and directing of patriotic programs. Action and good
works defined 100 per cent Americanism for the V.F.W. as the group
entered its fifty-fifth year.[62]

In the same year the Legion's Americanism Commission still appeared to be bothered by the phrase and the *American Legion Magazine* published an article which queried "What Is 100 Per Cent Americanism?" The author, Robert Pitkin, spoke for the Legion's Americanism Commission. Pitkin said that the term had long caused
trouble to the Legion and admitted that there had been pressure
within the organization itself to wipe the phrase from Legion speech.
This had been accomplished chiefly through ridicule, Pitkin complained. He concluded that even if it had taken many forms in the
past, the training of citizens for their tasks of citizenship encompassed
"everything the Legion meant by 100 per cent Americanism."[63] But
doubts lingered and as late as 1958, the Legion still felt constrained to
explain the phrase. The official monthly magazine complained that
100 per cent Americanism had been subject to criticism as "if it were
synonymous with zenophobia and isolation." No critic ever suggested
to the Legion what he thought the proper percentage of Americanism

might be, the editorial continued. Two aspects of 100 per cent Americanism, said the article, were the open and prideful display of love and loyalty to the American Government and the other was uncovering and exposing those who worked "secretly to overthrow the system." [64]

The Legion, D.A.V., and the V.F.W. found it easier to define the ideal of 100 per cent Americanism by enacting programs of Americanism over the years. The use of good works which materially benefited the recipients proved a more effective type of Americanism than words and definitions, they discovered.[65] The U.S.W.V., on the other hand, never questioned the 1926 official definition, and it continues to link the ideal of 100 per cent Americanism with the war service it performed in 1898.[66] Similarly, the M.O.W.W. indicated a generation after its founding that possession of a Federal commission still symbolized 100 per cent Americanism. In 1954 Major General Melvin Maas, former Commander-in-Chief of the M.O.W.W., deplored the military's alleged lack of prestige. The lack was due, said General Maas, to "a deliberate conspiracy" during the Cold War period. In the name of Americanism, General Maas told the Order that its task was to lead local communities and restore the military's reputation. He stated positively, but with few details, that once that happened the military could assume leadership of the country during the Cold War and end the conflict. Maas concluded his speech by echoing the familiar sentiments of Theodore Roosevelt in stating that Americanism meant a physically healthy race and the nation had gone soft: "We need that return of vigor of the old American stock. We must combat the machine-age in this respect. Fathers; look to your child. Avoid ease and pampering." [67]

Maas' pedestrian thoughts simply joined a long parade of similar statements for, despite the millions of words and thousands of dollars thrown out in attempts to isolate and capture it, the definition of Americanism has never been completely solved by a majority of the organized veterans' societies. The groups have tried to prove that Americanism has a fixed content which might be determined and defined. They have been aided mightily by the exigencies of tepid, hot and cold wars, but Americanism remains an abstraction which defies definition. In their perplexity over the question of Americanism, the larger veterans' associations often have turned to patriotic programs as a substitute. Action and deeds can speak more persuasively than words and what could be more in keeping with the idealized, albeit impatient, American character?

Chapter VI

CREATION OF AMERICANISM PROGRAMS

To most persons opposed to veterans' societies for varying reasons there is nothing positive to be said about their patriotic activities. Almost always it is the irresponsible statement, the disorderly convention-time antics, the selfish bonus raids upon the treasury, or the antisubversion tactics which conspire to give the critic his images of the veteran. These days, when military crises rain down upon us, let an ex-serviceman who organizes a private militia "to protect ourselves against the Reds" also be identified as a member of the V.F.W. or the Legion, and too many persons will conclude that such hysterical actions typify the group to which he belongs. It is incorrect to allow the words and deeds of individuals or even collections of individuals to symbolize an entire association of men and women. Frequently, authorized and unofficial personnel speaking in the name of the entire membership of a veterans' society, will cause an uproar by suggesting, for example, that anyone who opposes the building of fall-out shelters is a traitor. But does this reflect the views of all his fellow comrades? The chances are that they do not.

In order to understand how and why unofficial and official activities, policies, and pronouncements are created or remain stillborn, the internal administrative structure of a veterans' organization and the type of men who run it must be studied. Questions relating to the actual power held by the rank and file members also should be examined before judgment is passed upon the whole brotherhood. The programs of the veterans, by and large, receive great public acceptance, and in many rural areas the local post or encampment is the main social center. Thousands of activities are of immense value and aid to communities in every part of the nation. The operations are not perfect, of course, for they are so multitudinous and embrace such a vast scope of subjects that consistency of purpose and execution sometimes is lost. Also, there are the vagaries of the administrators which must be taken into account. They have sabotaged or subverted many a worthy enterprise, sometimes with intent but often through lack of imagination. A look at the Americanism programs' histories is necessary to fill in the picture of the veterans, for they show the ex-soldiers at their worst and certainly their best.

* * * *

With the exception of the Legion, most of the organized veterans' societies found that marshalling patriotic endeavors was a difficult job. Many members had always assumed that simply by virtue of being veterans they were more profoundly patriotic than the mass of citizenry and it was the latter who needed guidance from the former in matters of formal nationalism. Often, however, when the leaders of the groups attempted to initiate patriotic programs the biggest obstacle proved to be their own members and not the public. This was especially true among the Spanish-American War veterans who resolutely clung to the idea that their military service was the brightest badge of Americanism that one might wear and little else was needed as adornment. Such beliefs endowed the generation of ninety-eight with a fundamental individualism, but it undercut attempts by both organizations' administrators to formulate and enact large-scale patriotic projects. The V.F.W. and the U.S.W.V. copied the office of National Patriotic Instructor from the G.A.R. and the officers who held that post found that teaching patriotism was often a thankless job. From 1924 until 1935, the U.S.W.V.'s Patriotic Instructors discovered that local camps ignored the national office; reports were not submitted and the veterans were lax in showing respect for the flag. On the local level in 1935, the U.S.W.V.'s National Commandary found that patriotic activities were conducted largely by unqualified persons. The "physically and mentally down" too frequently were appointed camp patriotic leaders which resulted in the office becoming "ornamental." [1]

Although plagued by financial problems during the twenties and thirties, the V.F.W. appeared better organized than the U.S.W.V. Walter Joyce headed the patriotic division of the V.F.W. in this period and in 1925, he proudly stated that it was the pioneer organization in "Americanization." The group's chief goals were elimination of the hyphen, respect for the flag, and censorship of un-American textbooks. In its patriotic work, Joyce declared, the V.F.W. was securing the active co-operation of the Legion but he complained that so little money was available that the program might have to be halted. As if to bear him out, it was revealed by 1928 that two-thirds of all the V.F.W.'s Patriotic Instructors were inactive. [2] The organization's pa-

triotic program, however, bore some results. A booklet on flag etiquette
was distributed nationally in 1926. The V.F.W. claims that it was the
first patriotic society to compile such a tract. The Legion also produced
a similar pamphlet with the statement that adoption of a flag code
had been one of its earliest goals but the Legion has never boasted
that its booklet appeared first. The language of both codes is the
same. The two groups also co-operated in the twenties on a campaign
to have "The Star Spangled Banner" adopted as the nation's official
anthem, a movement the V.F.W. says it initiated. In 1931 the song
was made America's national anthem by Congress.[3]

The M.O.W.W., in contrast to the V.F.W. and Legion, inaugurated
no formal Americanism plan. Some members felt that performing
civic duties meant an extension of patriotic activities. For example,
a Chicago chapter reported in 1922 that it had offered to help local
governmental agencies maintain law and order in the gangster-torn
city. The M.O.W.W.'s actions in the realm of Americanism usually
depended upon the labors of one man or chapter, but, although the
Order saw its greatest responsibility in protecting America from
armed attack and internal subversion, it did organize two national
campaigns. April 6 was adopted as Army Day and a memorial service
known as "The Massing of the Colors" is held annually.[4]

For the first few years of its life the D.A.V. ignored patriotic programs but it did adopt a limited Americanism program in 1934.
First Junior Vice Commander Peter Nugent explained that, prior to
1934, the Legion's Americanism activities had been sufficient for the
D.A.V. since the two organizations had overlapping memberships.
By 1934, however, Nugent wished the D.A.V. to create its own program. He charged that a "fascist" group in Los Angeles, called the
Friends of New Germany, tried to subvert D.A.V. members and that
the Nazi society used a smokescreen of anti-Communist talk to pro-
pagate racial and religious hatred. In response, the D.A.V. organized
an Americanism Committee to combat the subversion which turned
its information over to the McCormack-Dickstein Congressional
investigation committee. Subsequent to this affair, however, the
D.A.V.'s Americanism group existed only for conventions.[5]

It remained for the Legion to demonstrate to the other veterans'
societies how Americanism programs should be organized. The 1919
Minneapolis national convention established the Legion's Americanism
Commission. The group hoped to realize the basic ideal of 100 per
cent Americanism through "the planning, establishment and conduct
of a continuous, constructive educational system" designed to:

"1. Combat all anti-American tendencies, activities and propaganda;

"2. Work for the education of immigrants, prospective American citizens and alien residents in the principles of Americanism;

"3. Inculcate the ideals of Americanism in the citizen population, particularly the basic American principle that the interests of all the people are above those of any special interest or any so-called class or section of the people;

"4. Spread throughout the people of the nation information as to the real nature and principles of American Government;

"5. Foster the teaching of Americanism in all schools." [6]

The Legion needed a national group to set patriotic policies. Local Legionnaires between 1919 and 1921, in the name of Americanism, often took the law into their own hands or arbitrarily discriminated against groups or individuals with whom they were not in sympathy. In the fall of 1919 the Austrian violinist Fritz Kreisler found his American engagements cancelled or picketed by local Legionnaires. In Astoria, Oregon, a newspaper editor was driven out of town by local Legionnaires who felt that he edited a communist paper. When labor unrest produced strikes in Cincinnati, Omaha, Youngstown and Detroit local Legion posts were so unfriendly that an *American Legion Weekly* editorial cautioned Legionnaires about usurping the duties of local civil authorities.[7] It asked posts to study the question of Americanism and be prepared to submit resolutions on the problem at the November, 1919 National Convention.[8]

Although plans were drawn up for the patriotic program, it failed to materialize. Money problems beset the Legion from late 1919 until 1921 and various activities were curtailed. The Americanism Commission's first meeting was held in January, 1920 under the fair-minded chairmanship of Arthur Woods, who based the program on what he hoped was an enlightened policy and who insisted that the Legion should set an example of law and order. He promised that the Legion's patriotic division would define Americanism in such a manner that it could not be open to any wrong construction. Since the hyphenated American was still the major obstacle to Woods' generation, the basic job of Americanism was education and the alien and the immigrant should benefit most from the program. Woods simply desired to inaugurate a policy of understanding in regard to foreigners.[9]

The program was first spelled out on June 3, 1921 in the pages of the *Weekly* and from it stems the Legion's present-day Americanism activities. The original plan was divided into three parts: "To Understand America," "To Know America," and "To Love America." "Fate had decreed that English shall be the language of the American people," the text of the program read, "therefore, English must be the only medium of instruction in the schools." The Legion stated that the program should be directed toward the new citizen so that he might more thoroughly comprehend America. As a result, under the title dealing with understanding America, the entire text was devoted to the English courses the immigrant should take. "Citizenship," the Americanism Commission stated, "was not a free gift."[10] In order to know America, the Commission announced that every student must take a course in American history and civics. It was necessary to realize that "America was built around the home, the school and the church." The Commission warned that "if these three cease to be, America will be no more." Loving America could be attained by knowing her; if America had some imperfections, it could be made perfect by good citizenship.[11]

Members of the Americanism Commission who had formulated the program included its paid director, Henry J. Ryan, Fiorello LaGuardia, and Colonel Gordon Johnston, former aide to General Leonard Wood. The plans they created became the framework for all future activities. Little by little, each national convention has added another activity, another subcommittee, or a new campaign. By 1957 of the Legion's twelve national commissions, the Americanism Commission ranked fifth in total expenditures. From 1924 to 1957 the Legion allocated between two and five per cent of its annual budgets to Americanism programs. The bulk, however, of the Legion's expenses were in the fields of administration, public relations, and publications.[12]

The Legion's success with its large Americanism activities attracted the attention of the V.F.W. leaders. In 1934 the Pennsylvania Republican politician James E. Van Zandt, who was National Commander, announced the formation of the V.F.W.'s Department of Americanism. A new program became necessary, said Van Zandt, due to the increased threat of subversion. "Beloved comrade" Walter Joyce was made chairman of the department and a young assistant, Victor E. Devereaux, became its director. Van Zandt and Devereaux assured the V.F.W. that the latter had prepared a militant Americanism program capable of "guiding" the nation's destiny.[13] The V.F.W.'s plan was basically a copy of the Legion's program, but on a smaller scale.

Its scope has remained less extensive, although the V.F.W. includes national defense affairs in its Americanism programs while the Legion does not.

By 1961 the two largest veterans' societies reached into almost every American community with their Americanism activities. Both the programs are divided roughly into five major fields, each of which, in turn, is sub-divided. The primary divisions are: Community Service and Safety Activities; Immigration, Naturalization and Citizenship; Education; Recreation and Athletics; and Un-American and Subversive activities.[14] In addition to the major groups, standing committees are created for special functions. Such committees in the Legion are: Law and Order; Religious Emphasis; Accident Prevention; Joint Committee of the American Legion and the National Education Association; Marksmanship; Boys State; Sons of the American Legion; and Un-American Activities.[15] The Legion's entire program contains almost fifty specialized projects which run the gamut from high school driver training courses and oratorical contests to maintenance of confidential files; and from Back to God campaigns to organized baseball leagues.[16]

Americanism activities are best understood in light of the Legion's federal structure. The lowest unit within the society is the post which obtains an organizational charter from national headquarters. Posts organize in the states to form departments with one department for each state and territory. At the top of the Legion's organizational edifice presides the National Commander and the ten national officers who are the five national vice commanders, an adjutant, a judge advocate, a chaplain, a historian, and a treasurer.[17] The single most powerful committee in the Legion's hierarchy is the National Executive Committee (N.E.C.) which works more closely with the Americanism Commission than any other Legion administrative body. The N.E.C. is composed of the National Commander, the five national vice commanders, the chaplain, and the adjutant. In addition, there is a member from each department and all past national commanders are *ex officio* members. The N.E.C.'s job is to carry on the Legion's organizational details between the annual national conventions. At a minimum, it meets three times a year.[18] The N.E.C. holds a veto power over all appointments to any of the twelve national commissions' offices. As an example, the Americanism Commission's chairman and its paid personnel all must be approved by the N.E.C. In 1948 former Americanism Commission member Justin Gray claimed that relations between the N.E.C. and the Americanism group were

extremely close. Gray said that the liason at that time gave the
Americanism Commission more influence in high Legion circles than
any other national commission.[19]

There is no doubt that the Commission's influence can be pervasive
when the need arises. Its programs and organization are duplicated
on every level for each post and department maintains its own Americanism Committee. The departmental committees are composed of
men representing each state congressional district. Like the national
commission, the departmental committees are divided into subcom-
mittees.[20] On the post level the organization is much the same as in
the departments. The posts' membership sizes determine the scope
of the activities. Although in theory the posts and departments have
independence of action, they cannot authorize any programs of which
the national commission disapproves.[21]

The national headquarters has generally tried to make the programs
appear cohesive. It directs operations and policies by convention
mandates. In the case of Americanism activities, the Americanism
Commission indicates approval of certain resolutions which are given
to a convention committee before being presented to the delegates.
The resolutions committee specifies which proposals its chairman
thinks should be accepted and invariably they are adopted. Superficially, it appears that the approval indicates the entire Legion's
assent to the mandates but such approbation is deceiving as events
in some cases show.[22]

One reason why the national conventions rarely contradict headquarter's sponsored policies lies in the nature of the Legion's political
structure which bears quite a resemblance to the two national political
parties. Direct suffrage for the election of national officers does not
exist in the organization since the post Legionnaire cannot directly
vote for the delegate of his choice to attend the national convention.
Instead, he votes for a representative who first attends a county
convention. The county convention chooses delegates to the departmental convention who, in turn, select the national convention delegates. Legionnaire critics of the system have charged that it obstructs
the direct presentation of the average Legionnaire's wishes. One
Legionnaire commented in 1945 that his post activities were run by
a small, interested group which the rank and file allowed to direct
all post affairs, including selection of delegates to the county conventions. At the county and departmental assemblies the process was
repeated. All such criticisms apparently are true enough, but again

it must be pointed out that the Legion is hardly unique in these respects.[23]

Obviously, the national conventions often tend to be affairs that rubber stamp official views, and in the area of the Americanism programs, these practices are only one way in which the activities appear to be made cohesive. Headquarters also implement policy by the use of a fulltime, professional Americanism staff which executes the Americanism Commission's directives. The regular Commission, since 1924, has consisted of twenty-four national executive officers who meet semi-annually with the N.E.C. Their decisions have been put into operation by the program's director and his assistants. The number of professional staffmen varies yearly but the average is six with each of these assistants being assigned as an expert in a particular field. As an example, in 1945, a Legionnaire school teacher was given the job of running the Commission's educational affairs. His main job was to compile evidence of subversion in school textbooks.[24]

The structure of the other veterans' organizations is basically the same as the Legion's but none of them retain as large a professional Americanism staff. The V.F.W.'s Americanism and Community Service Department, as an example, which has the only other Legion-type program, exists with three paid directors and three stenographers. The Department serves mainly as a coordinating agency that disseminates information and material, for apparently, due to the agency's nature, it cannot exercise the control over local Americanism activities that the Legion's commission does. V.F.W. records have failed to reveal how much policy originates within the Americanism Department. Brochures, monographs, and convention reports indicate that the division reflects more policy than it creates and there have been no instances where the Americanism Department reversed official policy declarations.[25] The V.F.W. has duplicated most of the Legion's activities. Its main innovation has been the inclusion of an American sovereignty campaign that is designed specifically to counter the work of the United World Federalists and similar organizations.[26]

The philosophy and purpose that guides the V.F.W.'s and Legion's Americanism programs must be fully comprehended to evaluate them. Americanism work is far from being purely idealistic. As early as 1920 a publicity conscious element took control in the Legion. Its second National Commander, Frederick William Galbraith, was described by publicist Marquis James as the "best publicity man for a cause" since Theodore Roosevelt. Galbraith sought to obtain public good will realizing that the Legion, as a minority organization, could not function without it. In doing so, he set the tone for subsequent Legion activity and by 1920, the Cleveland convention heard the Americanism Commission propose a national director of publicity whose job would be to "conduct American propaganda."[27]

In 1924 John C. Quinn, Commission Chairman, told the St. Paul convention that his work depended upon public acceptance of the Legion. One function of the Americanism Commission was to create favorable public sentiment on the Legion's behalf. Once the citizens' support was obtained, Legion backed issues could be presented and it was hoped that the Commission's good will efforts might help persuade people to support Legion policies. The publicity value of the Americanism Commission's community service programs possessed additional merits for they not only won the Legion respect but attracted more members. The larger the Legion's ranks were, the stronger the national organization was.[28] The Commission's chairman in 1925, Frank C. Cross, more bluntly outlined the spirit of the Americanism work. The Commission itself was a sales unit committed to "sell the ideas of the Legion" to the country. The citizens were apathetic to the monotonous appeals of patriotic exhorters and individual Legionnaires under the guidance of the Commission were to dissipate apathy by "retailing the spirit of Americanism."[29] This patriotic sales pitch, in one case, took the indirect form of Junior Baseball which the Legion has zestfully sponsored since 1925. The Commission discovered the obvious fact that baseball was extremely popular with adults and children so the game served the dual purpose of building sportsmanship while gaining members and support for the Legion.[30]

The V.F.W., meanwhile, tried the same approach as the Legion by supporting movements for the creation and maintenance of playgrounds. Patriotic Instructor Walter Joyce claimed, in 1925, that both community service programs and counter subversive activities earned the organization a good reputation. For that matter, continually during the past thirty-five years, both organizations have officially stipulated in their Americanism manuals and pamphlets that community work and sports activities have given the veterans a positive, civic-minded public image that enlisted members and sold the national groups' policies, a point of view happily sanctioned in 1953 by the Americanism Commission in a national report.[31]

Community service activities are interlaced with education and immigration programs and are among the oldest and largest activities sponsored by the Legion and V.F.W. There is less to criticize in these fields than in other aspects of the Americanism programs;

moreover, critics of the veterans' societies often have ignored the positive contributions made to the life of the communities involved, for undoubtedly such projects represent some of the more commendable features of Americanism work.[32] In 1954 both the Legion and the V.F.W. claimed that their civic programs had reached and benefited millions. They had backed 'teen-age council groups, sponsored golf tournaments, instituted voting drives, opened recreation parks, and initiated and maintained health camps for undernourished children. During the depression the two societies accomplished outstanding achievements. Between 1938 and 1939 the Legion spent almost seven million dollars on aid to needy children while the V.F.W. started hundreds of youth projects to aid adolescents and thus combat radicalism among jobless young people.[33] After the Second World War the Legion continued its good work by converting abandoned barracks into temporary housing for veterans.[34]

In a few respects the record in community service is marred. Both the Legion and the V.F.W. obviously equate salesmanship of their ideologies with a healthy community and blatantly retail their patriotic principles to attract numbers and gain more power to enforce their will. While this method has been excellent from their viewpoint as a recruiting and publicity device, it has been essentially a restricted if practical form of patriotism.[35] One other aspect of this area of criticism is revealed in its "Back to God Movement" which takes varied forms ranging from religious services to censorship of public morals. In the spirit that American traditions and values are derived from God, which all veterans' societies assert, the Legion institutionalized religious patriotism in 1950.

The ostensible purpose of the campaign is to improve the moral health of Americans, but in practice the plan often has tried to gain the Legion publicity and sanction its ideals and policies by religious identification. As an example, the Sunday nearest February 3 is officially designated "Four Chaplains Day" and is designed to encourage church-going. The service commemorates an inspiring and symbolic wartime religious event with emphasis on the Legionnaires' role as warriors and religious patriots. In 1955 local posts were directed to sponsor the ceremony and "obtain publicity using the name of the Post" locally involved.[36] Enforced conformity also has become a part of the "Back to God" campaign. In the name of moral decency the Legion wanted to censor various publications, but *Publisher's Weekly* strongly protested and acidly inquired why the Legion's concept of decency was necessarily superior to other groups.

Attempts have been made, as well, in another form of censorship to control and supervise the content of religious services within the Legion itself and one chaplain complained that any extemporaneous prayers were forbidden. Upon inquiry, officials implied that he should conform and that non-controversial, authorized prayers were available which were the only ones to be used.[37]

Another project, Junior Baseball, a part of the organization's multi-tudinous community service, also contains some flaws. Both major leagues and the Ford Motor Company have helped to underwrite the program and the Legion proudly reports that one million boys participate annually. During the 1953 season, the Legion stated that 275 former Junior Baseball players appeared in the major leagues, thanks to the Legionnaires. But the strain of racism has besmirched the sunny official portrait, for in the South, unhappily, the program has had to make allowance for racial bias. Tournament finals are usually held there, because southern mill towns provide larger crowds than in the North. No Negroes on northern Legion championship teams have been allowed to play in southern states. In 1948 a member of the Americanism Commission questioned this policy and was told by a fellow Commission member that white southern prejudices had to be respected or the Legion would be forced to drop Junior Base-ball in the South. What type of Americanism this policy represented has never been officially explained by Legion leaders.[38]

Although they attempt to broaden civic responsibilities among the citizenry and to sanctify organizational programs by identifying them with the Almighty, the obvious criticism of the Legion's and V.F.W.'s community service projects is their air of hypocrisy. While this charge is often true, it is partially unfair and unrealistic to let it stand at that. Both the Legion and the V.F.W. have analyzed the theoretical problem of Americanism. By its nature, it is an amorphous concept defying definition and attempts to give it a fixed content. It is difficult for the leaders of a veterans' organization, let alone the average member, to grasp the subtleties of Americanism. The two major societies logically have translated the abstraction into a series of tangible programs and plans with the result that Americanism activi-ties have become practical, understandable, and manageable. The Legion's and V.F.W.'s motives behind their indirect approaches might be questioned but criticism should be moderated in view of the various projects' accomplishments which sometimes deserve more praise than censure.

The programs' effectiveness in promulgating national policies is hard to evaluate. Do community service projects truly sell the societies' points of view? Despite the Legion's conclusions no evidence exists indicating that they do. Undoubtedly the two major veterans' organizations have obtained a great deal of good will and community acceptance from their projects. But, as an example, no records show that Junior Baseball players support Legion policy in gratitude for the athletic program.

There are other fields such as education, where the Americanism programs might have produced a greater ideological impact and possibly more criticism. Despite the catholicity of community service work, education undoubtedly is of the greatest importance to the veterans and all of the groups have carefully and narrowly watched the schools of America. In the Legion's case, education has formed the basis of indoctrination in Americanism with its original educational activities centered on removal of the hyphen. By 1923 it had moved beyond this concept and a History Investigating Committee was organized. The Legion and the V.F.W. claimed that history should be utilized to set examples of patriotic and civic character. Books that contained derogatory statements about national heroes, even "if truthful," should be abolished, for pupils were too immature to accept the facts that prominent Americans could have made blunders or mistakes.[39] Similar attitudes are not confined to the Legion and the V.F.W. alone. The U.S.W.V. has been on record since 1924 demanding that all teachers take the same strict oath of allegiance as military personnel. The D.A.V. wished to make the teaching of Americanism mandatory and during the Second World War it asked that the Federal Government enforce such a requirement. Since the First World War, all of the veterans' societies have had extensive contact with local school systems. Recommended books, flags, placards, creeds of Americanism, and official oaths of allegiance have been either donated or forced upon the schools by the organized veterans.[40]

Teachers and institutions that depart from the societies' views on Americanism have become the targets of attacks and economic interpretations found in textbooks are of special concern to them. In the twenties, the V.F.W. and the Legion demanded that Professor Harold O. Rugg's history textbooks be withdrawn from circulation because he allegedly attacked free enterprise by suggesting that advertising added costs to the consumer. Many school systems obliged the veterans. Flag education programs and national essay contests were instituted by the patriotic groups and when educators criticized such activities they were quickly condemned. Columbia Teacher's College became the traditional *béte noire* of American education to the veterans along with many non-veterans. The Legion charged that Teacher's College graduates formulated "vague socialistic" theories and passed them on to students.[41] In 1949 the Legion declared that American history teachers had no right to instruct unless they believed "without reservation in American free enterprise and the dignity and worth of the individual." A writer in the Legion's magazine charged also in 1949 that too many teachers were debunkers or were "too judicially minded" and tended to "play down" American accomplishments. The Americanism Commission reiterated the same view in 1954.[42]

The Legion did discover an example of an ideal educator in 1951 by singling out Paul Wamsley, principal of Public School Number 51 of Buffalo, New York. P.S. 51 was not a progressive school whose teaching methods were subject to continual change. The school stressed Americanism with a vengeance in every class. In history courses the students studied American heroes; in English classes they studied American historical documents; music classes sang patriotic songs and, unsurprisingly, the art courses used perhaps more red, white and blue crayons than any other type. Wamsley's administration of education was patriotic and nationalistic and because of this, a Legion spokesman rated the school as superior while noting with pride that the principal was an active Legionnaire.[43] To the Legion and other veterans, the word individualism is almost synonymous with Americanism and Wamsley's patriotic program also symbolized an individualistic attack on educational centralism which the veterans fearfully regard as creeping socialism. In recent years, both the M.O.W.W. and the Legion have vehemently criticized federal aid to education arguing that federal funds lead to centralized thought control. The Legion has also managed to link progressive educationist theories with federal aid. An article in the monthly magazine stated, perhaps rightly enough, that educationists formed cliques who dominated national education policies. If the educationists obtained federal money, they would solidify their control over educational policies.[44]

Unfortunately for those who delight in criticizing the veterans, not all of the latters' objections to the American school systems are baseless even if the patriots' remedies are questionable. Too, in years past various of the societies have materially aided some schools. During the depression both the V.F.W. and the Legion gave money to faltering educational systems and provided equipment as well as scholarships. Even the Legion's arch critic, Professor William Gellermann, admitted that he often found excellent relations between Legionnaires and local schools. He correctly decided that the trouble lay in national policies issued from Indianapolis.[45]

The most dangerous aspect of the veterans' educational programs often is that they produce conformity. If a school receives help from the V.F.W. or the Legion, it is expected to promulgate the societies' concepts of Americanism. The veterans' groups have stated that they wish Americans to study civic and national affairs but in practice they accept only conventional views of which the national headquarters approve and examinations of troublesome social problems are ignored. As an example in American history, Grant's generosity to Lee and not the Emancipation Proclamation with its divisive and complex aftermath, symbolizes the traumatic Civil War to the Legion. In educational affairs, the field of history is pragmatically utilized largely for its symbolic value and the images selected are those that could be identified with the patriotic societies themselves. History, as a result, consists of military exploits by brave men and military heroism serves to illustrate character while embossing the veterans with a special patina in their own eyes. War service of any type suffices to make the ex-servicemen patriots, thus patriotism and leadership have become one and inseparable to the societies. Leaders whose patriotism could not be questioned have been able to assume the role of experts in any field that strikes their fancy.[46]

Closely allied with the vexations of education are the problems of immigration which are connected in the official views of the veterans. The Legion's Americanism Commission has stated that the goal of every immigrant should be conformity to American culture and most of the support it gave to local schools and adult classes during the twenties centered on this theory.[47] Behind this reasoning lay the feeling that the melting-pot had failed. Because of the failure, the patriotic societies determined to launch a dual campaign; they fanned the flames under the melting-pot by use of 100 per cent Americanism in the schools, and at the same time, they endorsed restricted immigration in the hope that the aliens already in the United States might be assimilated.[48]

At first, particularly in 1921, veterans often followed deviating lines in regard to Americanizing the immigrant. In the Legion, National Headquarters initially expressed one view while individual Legionnaires were urged to welcome the immigrant and appreciate the cultural heritage he represented since the Americanism Commission's policy was social justice and fair play. The immigrant was expected to learn English, but only as an economic and expeditious tool to aid him.[49] Legionnaires, meanwhile, acted without regard to official views. In some cases they extended friendship to immigrants and hyphenated Americans. For example, a Minnesota Legionnaire defended the right of German-American Lutherans to conduct church services in German. By contrast, however, an ex-soldier in Oklahoma referred to a German-American settlement as a "Boche community." The wife of one Legion member expressed fear over hordes of immigrants who were both an economic danger and a health problem.[50] The official emphasis shifted and became more militant by 1924. Increasingly, the immigrant was expected to embrace all American cultural values and completely discard those of his native country. The Legion demanded that no school courses be taught in any language but English, explaining that Americanization meant stimulating patriotism and better citizenship among the newly naturalized through the medium of the English language. At no time did the Legion express the least appreciation for the culture that the immigrant brought with him.[51]

The Legion claimed a partial victory in the enactment of the 1924 National Origins Act. Since 1920 it had asked the Government to amend the immigration laws, contending that too many illiterate and impoverished immigrants arrived in America only to become liabilities. Republican Senator Henry Cabot Lodge supported the Legion's views. He told its members that the European alien must be made to think of his adopted home first, because if he did not, he would harken to old political loyalties at home and thus embroil America in European affairs. In regard to Asians during the same period, V. S. McClatchy, a California publisher with racist views concerning orientals, warned in the pages of the Legion's *Weekly* of the dangers found among unassimilative Japanese labor.[52] Under the National Origins Act, the Federal Government was given the impossible task of trying to determine the ethnic origins of the American people. On the basis of its analysis, the Government did fix quotas for immigration based on the supposed national origins of its citizens. The result was a racist's victory with predictable effects for the act doubled the quota from Great Britain while it halved Ireland's and Germany's. The Scandinavian quotas were cut by two-thirds, immigration from southern Europe was almost abolished and orientals were virtually excluded.[53]

The Legion has found no fault with its immigration policies since the enactment of the 1924 National Origins bill. In 1954 its Americanism Commission reminded the public that it always had opposed an influx of immigrants. In line with that view, the Legion fully supported the 1952 McCarran-Walter Immigration Act. The Legion correctly pointed out that the McCarran bill introduced no new concepts of immigration policy and that it embodied traditional American immigration practices stemming from the 1924 National Origins Act. Basically, the McCarran-Walter bill codified all existing immigration statutes and made the lawyer's job easier.[54]

All of the veterans' societies have followed the Legion's stand on immigration. In 1930 the D.A.V. heard immigrants described as "riffraff" who sought American jobs. The M.O.W.W.'s National Adjutant in 1931 wanted legislation allowing only natural born citizens to run for or be appointed to any public office. After the Second World War, the veterans' societies passed resolutions that barred displaced persons from entering the United States generally expressing the fear that Communism would enter the country with these persons. There was public criticism of this stand and, in 1953, the Legion unexpectedly modified its position. The Americanism Commission announced that America should accept 400,000 refugees as her "fair share." [55]

The worst charge brought against the veterans in regard to immigration is that their policies are and have been racist and there seems to be conclusive evidence to support the allegations. The National Origins Act was so discriminatory against orientals, for example, that it damaged American diplomatic relations with Japan for a generation. The veterans' societies, especially the Legion, have long maintained relations with groups who advocated oriental exclusion and studies show that the nature of the protests against the Asians were often racist.[56] During World War II, the Legion demanded that no immigration quotas be scrapped until all veterans had found jobs. The California Department objected to the official viewpoint and passed a resolution asking that Chinese quotas be repealed. The Californians stated that the Chinese were American allies and removal of the quotas would counter Japanese propaganda which emphasized American racial bias. Representative Warren Magnuson, Democrat from Washington and a Legionnaire, introduced such a bill in Congress with Past National Commander Louis Johnson publicly supporting him. On November 1, 1943, the Legion suddenly reversed its stand without explanation.[57]

The patriots have always stated that only total Americanization of the immigrant is acceptable. Behind this policy lies the assumption that Americans society and institutions are practically perfect. The veteran's groups' concept of American culture is bascially Anglo-Saxon and they exhibit fear mixed with contempt or condescension for the immigrant's culture. They have always suspected that the foreign-born might alter native American society in a drastic fashion. The effects of Americanization work, however, have been questionable despite all the energy, money and effort put into it.[58]

There are Legion records that show Americanization has been resented by immigrants despite all attempts to make it palatable. A French war bride, having resided in America for twenty months after World War I, wrote in the Legion's *Weekly* that aliens would always love their homelands if they had emigrated as adults. In Americans they found "a presumed superiority" and as a result the elder immigrants stayed together for cultural security. Americanization efforts to break the alien's foreign ties caused resentment. She hoped in the future that such work could be done tactfully.[59]

Perhaps American ethnic nationalism has been intensified by the veterans' Americanism efforts. There is a curious relationship between the patriotic societies' policies and racial chauvinism. Both the veterans' organizations and the hyphenated nationalists are special interest groups and it is probable, as some historians claim, that the growth of such organizations symbolize the social dislocation of American society. The veterans have wished to preserve what they imagine is a traditional culture in the midst of change, but often their Americanization policies and programs have culminated in the accentuation of cultural differences.[60]

Many immigrants, however, have received material benefits from the Americanization activities. Local veterans' posts and encampments often have extended welcoming ceremonies to new citizens and the veterans have provided free legal advice and naturalization classes for foreigners. The new citizen, however, initially only learned about American history from the veterans' point of view. In 1954 the Legion's Americanism Commission advised Legion posts on the type of instructors they should employ. It said that no teachers should be retained who "are doubtful or pessimistic about the benefits of our form of government or who feel it necessary to stress the frailties and shortcomings of our national heroes and national leaders." This, of course, was entirely consistent with the Legion's usual circumscribed views on all American educational policies.[61]

In fairness, it must be said that the rank and file veterans too often are blamed for official actions. Much welfare work is local and spontaneous but when it comes to the attention of the national headquarters the purpose of the project becomes a public relations tool.

In 1936 Legion sponsored naturalization ceremonies were inaugurated in Philadelphia. National headquarters favorably evaluated the public relations effect of the program with the result that the ceremonies have been officially institutionalized for the entire Legion with the warning that post leadership should be unobtrusive but influential in the type of instruction given the new citizens.[62]

What can be said concerning these extensive community programs? As special interest groups the goals of the veterans have been pragmatic and they have thought and acted in the conviction that their views on Americanism were entirely in the national interest. The effects, however, of the Americanism programs have been mixed. It is true that millions of people have received extensive aid, but it is impossible to ascertain if the recipients of community service projects have bothered to subscribe to official views because of the help. Possibly, the schools have been affected the most by the Americanism programs. While they have been helped in a material sense, in exchange, the societies have tried in various communities to force their official beliefs onto the teachers and administrators. Education, too often to the veterans, means indoctrination and not examination.

The result of all such actions, whether in education, religion, or immigration, inevitably leads to rigidity of thought precisely at the moment of history when America must, if the society is to survive, produce viable, flexibly-minded citizens. Undoubtedly, a true knowledge of one's heritage may be of real importance in fashioning the responsible adult of tomorrow. While the veterans do excellent work in acquainting youngsters and immigrants with the fundamentals of civics, a true knowledge of our heritage is exactly what they deny them. The bad as well as the good in the democratic heritage must be acknowledged if such a community is to be realistic. To ignore past errors and old faults is to incorporate weaknesses into the system which will certainly guarantee its collapse under the pressures of the future.

CHAPTER VII

COUNTER SUBVERSION AND AUTHORITARIANISM

A surprising number of Americans consider themselves to be infallible in regard to three very complex subjects: weather, education, and loyalty. Unsurprisingly the veterans, and those who sit in judgment on them, fight most heatedly about the last issue. Both sides declare that patriotism means love of country, but the veterans' critics charge that too many of the ex-servicemen use hatred in the guise of nationalism. Indeed, much of the programming and activity carried on under the banner of pro-Americanism has been and is currently directed against a welter of events, topics and doctrines disagreeable to the veterans, but all labeled as Marxist.

Persons who are suspicious of the patriots' motives point to Sino-Russian tension and hopefully say that Communism today might be weakening as an international power bloc and that within the United States its followers have never been so few and ineffective. But to the majority of veterans' societies the picture is still insidious, for it is what is at hand that concerns them and the very diminutiveness of the Communist Party of America makes it just that more difficult to combat. Once the physical manifestations of the international conspiracy within our midst are removed the menace becomes doubled, for then citizens must fight ghostly abstractions which frequently take the form of ideas or beliefs measured and found wanting against the single standard of Americanism. In such a dark, suspicious atmosphere, the faultfinders say the veterans disguise prejudices and personal fears about the society around them and sublimate their negative reactions in the name of patriotism. This gloomy portrayal may certainly be true enough in many respects, but two questions are rarely asked by those who dislike the martial fraternities and their concepts of national loyalty. Do the views held by the ex-soldiers represent an aberrant point of view from the rest of the public's? And, again, do the voices and policies of a few speak for many? A scrutiny of the recent past raises some questions which are not easily answered.

* * *

Counter subversive activities usually earn the veterans' societies more notoriety than praise because the taint of authoritarianism and irresponsibility clings to many of the methods used in such practices. In the Legion, from 1919 until 1947, projects that combatted un-Americanism often were not centrally controlled activities within the Americanism program. On the contrary, work done in the name of counter subversion was often the action of a post, a small group within a post, or only one person at national headquarters. The un-Americanism efforts, however, carried the national organization's name. As an example, counter subversion programs from 1936 until 1945 were headed by Homer Chaillaux whose conception of Americanism was limited and narrow. For instance, he hated organized labor, which he considered subversive. Chaillaux spoke in the Legion's name, yet, as he did so, 100,000 Legionnaires who were trade union members began to coalesce in 1938 within the organization to liberalize Legion labor policies. It was Chaillaux, located at national headquarters, who was heard by the public, while the widely dispersed union Legionnaires were not. As a result, the impression was given that the entire Legion was antiunion. In such a respect, the larger veterans' societies are the victims of their own publicity consciousness as they often self-righteously advertise their patriotic virtues.[1]

The Chaillaux-type Americanism, unfortunately, seems to mark most of the patriots' counter subversive activities over the years. Basically, and not unnaturally, the groups have formulated their programs and actions on the assumption that an international plot existed to pervert or destroy the American heritage.[2] The veterans have lived in a world of shifting values and social change, a type of dislocation they dislike. The groups state that their war service plus traditional American social and economic institutions have been the factors which have made the country great, and they seek to keep her great by a militant protection of this heritage. They feel that four wars within sixty-two years have tested the veterans' defensive capabilities. But the wars also have conditioned and produced the veterans' concept of nationalism, which is a militaristic view harkening back to Theodore Roosevelt's 1918 Americanism. Any unconventional beliefs are officially regarded with suspicion. What is good for the veterans' groups is good for America. On some occasions, official statements and counter subversive projects have seemed authoritarian to liberal critics and, as the veterans' history of counter subversive activities is examined, it appears that there is much to support such a contention. Closer analysis, however, casts some doubt on such sweeping allegations.[3]

Truly, the record has not been auspicious. The same weary themes in counter subversion reappear with monotony from World War I to the present. Foreigners, pacifists, and advocates of international government have been the veterans' main targets. Liberals as a group, be they professors, politicians, union leaders or even other veterans, have also been attacked, for organized veterans are suspicious of the dissent inherent in liberalism and seem unable to accept diverging points of view. While it often appears that official policy is directed against a class, profession or group, as in the case of Chaillaux and the unions, in actuality, opposition is usually aimed at what the group or profession seem to represent rather than what they are. Ironically, conservative Supreme Court Justice Felix Frankfurter when a professor at the Harvard Law School opposed Federal prosecution of alleged Marxists in 1921, for which he was severely criticized by the M.O.W.W. The entire Harvard Law School, thanks to Frankfurter, thus was a hotbed of radicalism, according to the Order's official view.[4] M.O.W.W. chapters also have sent observers to suspicious public gatherings to take down names and forward them to national headquarters. In the twenties, their members dogged the footsteps of such alleged pacifists as Bertrand Russell and Senator William Borah of Idaho. In 1959 the Madison, Wisconsin chapter still was acting in the same tradition. A member wrote the M.O.W.W.'s *Bulletin* that he attended all the political meetings and guest lectures at the University of Wisconsin. With prideful eagerness, he recounted how he questioned socialist speakers and sent reports on them to the House Un-American Activities Committee.[5]

The Legion's forays into counter subversion have been famous among its liberal critics such as Norman Hapgood, who in 1926 told how a Concord, Massachusetts post broke up a pacifist meeting by means of physical violence. Two professors lost their jobs at a college in West Chester, Pennsylvania in 1927, thanks to a Legion post. The men had had the temerity to criticize American foreign policy in the pages of a local newspaper. During the depression, local Legionnaires often violently resisted union attempts to organize workers. El Centro, California's Legion post, in 1934, bitterly fought union members in the name of Americanism while in the same year Chaillaux signed a public advertisement in San Francisco newspapers that called the bloody longshoremen's strike un-American.[6] In addition, former Legion Americanism Commission member, Justin Gray, charged in 1948 that Chaillaux had used labor-baiting pamphlets and received support from hate groups such as Joseph P. Kamp's *Join the C.I.O. and Help Build* a *Soviet America* and George W. Blakely's society, the National Voters League for the Preservation of American Ideals.[7]

How much are the actions of several men to be regarded as the will of the total membership? Some liberals have indicted entire veterans' organizations as fascist due to their Americanism activities, among whom was William Gellermann, whose book on the Legion appeared in the late thirties. Individual action within the societies has seemed to bear out such an allegation. In 1934 a Congressional committee investigated fascist propaganda in the United States and found that two New England Legion department commanders started plans for a national political coup. They intended to replace President Franklin Roosevelt with retired Marine Corps Major General Smedley Butler. Butler, a crusty sort, scathingly refused the offer.[8] In 1941 former Legion national commander E. E. Spafford was publicly accused by his wife of being pro-Nazi in his views. During an interview Spafford unabashedly defended Adolph Hitler. And Spafford was not the only Legionnaire suspected of Nazi sympathies. One of the Legion's founders, New York Republican Representative Hamilton Fish, Jr., was censured by the 1943 Omaha convention for abuse of his Congressional franking privilege by spreading Nazi propaganda. Fish, in defense, called the sponsor of his censure resolution Jewish.[9]

What critics of the patriotic groups have failed to note is the number of cases where there has been opposition within the patriots' ranks over official or local policy. The M.O.W.W.'s local chapters spied on persons they suspected of radicalism, yet in 1932, Admiral R. R. Belknap, one of the Order's founders, protested against such actions. No one may ascertain how effective Belknap's protests were, but it signified some lack of harmony among the leaders of the M.O.W.W.[10] In 1941 the D.A.V.'s Americanism chairman, Major William J. McCluskey, titillated an audience of veterans as he luridly warned of a Negro uprising in America. The talk was tinged with racism, but in practice the D.A.V. has continued to treat all disabled applicants for help without regard to race. McCluskey's remarks are a part of the official records of the D.A.V., but not symbolic of its actual performance.[11] One of the worst blots on the societies' records was their official stand on the 1942 West Coast Japanese evacuation. There was, however, dissension within the groups over this policy, as indicated by a University of Chicago professor, Morton Grodzins, who published an extensive study, in 1949, of the role played by the veterans. They all backed the evacuation move and much of their reasoning was racist in nature. The Legion, particularly, was in the forefront of the campaign. Still, when the Hood River, Oregon Legion post struck sixteen names of Nisei veterans off its rolls, National Headquarters bowed to pressure and ordered them reinstated.[12]

Since World War II other incidents have occurred also wherein dissent and disagreement over national or local post policies erupted from the ranks of ex-servicemen. A prime example occurred in the V.F.W. in 1954. Post 603 of Norwalk, Connecticut announced in January, 1954 that it had embarked on a counter subversion campaign and its members were told to seek out suspected leftists and send reports on them to the F.B.I. *The Reporter Magazine* commissioned George W. Groh to interview the V.F.W. comrades. He discovered that the campaign was being conducted by just a few post personnel; only seventy-seven members out of a group of 350 attended the meeting when the movement was organized. Groh also found that not all the members present had concurred. National headquarters was equivocal concerning the incident and at the Philadelphia national encampment, the delegates approved of a V.F.W. and F.B.I. liaison, but the Norwalk affair was not discussed at great length.[13]

On the surface, such incidents appear authoritarian in nature. The charge of authoritarianism, however, must be approached carefully. The organized veteranas in recent years have a joint membership of approximately four million. The label of authoritarianism could not fit each and every member of a veterans' society. Dissent from official policies illustrates that fact, as does local disagreement over post policy.

Another reason for the trouble in ascertaining the degree of authoritarianism within the societies lies in definition. The term has different meanings to two generations. Gellermann, Justin Gray, and others who criticized patriotic groups were conditioned by the political and social events of the thirties. To the liberals of that era, authoritarianism meant Hitler's Germany or Mussolini's Italy whereas more sophisticated interpretations have appeared since 1945. Observers of Nazi methods were impressed and frightened by its ruthlessness and supposed efficiency. Occasionally, some Americans, such as the Legion's 1922 National Commander, Alvin Owsley, commented favorably on the fascist governments. Liberals were apt to interpret such a statement as proof of the Legion's fascistic tendencies which they also did when officials of veterans' societies, such as Chaillaux, used hate-mongering literature.[14] Some, like Gellermann, envisioned a sinister connection between the Legion's militarism and authoritarian practices. The war against the Axis Powers intensified liberal suspicions of authoritarianism and the veterans' societies and the 1944 Hood River Nisei incident seemed to confirm apprehensions about the organizations. Nazi cruelty disgusted Americans, but to many our wartime race riots and minority group discrimination were almost analogous. As the war ended, social scientists began behavioral analyses of authoritarian traits in American society.[15]

Between 1945 and 1950 a series of sociological and psychological studies on the subject appeared. Among the best known were those compiled by T. W. Adorno, F. H. Sanford, and H. W. Metz. None of the surveys can be called definitive. At first glance, however, the mass of statistics show that authoritarianism exists in America. The results, furthermore, appear to apply to many persons who speak for the veterans' groups.[16] The studies generally arrive at the same conclusion in ascertaining what constitutes authoritarianism. The best known of these was conducted by T. W. Adorno, who used a statistical scale to measure the degrees of authoritarianism. The ultimate gradient was fascism itself, hence the measurement was called the "F Scale."

Adorno concluded that the authoritarian personality possesses the ideas and skills typical of a highly industrialized society which are, at the same time, combined with anti-rational beliefs. He is both enlightened and superstitious; proud to be an individualist and fearful of not conforming. The authoritarian is jealous of his independence, but inclined to submit blindly to authority.[17] He holds rigid adherence to middle-class values; he is uncritical of traditional moral authorities; and he displays tendencies to punish people who violate conventional ideals. Often the authoritarian thinks in rigid categories and stereotypes and is disposed to feel that wild and dangerous plots abound in the world at large. According to Adorno, the authoritarian possesses a generalized hostility which takes the form of vilification against those he fears or resents. In regard to his leaders, he admires those who emphasize the visible benefits of membership in their group for he is concerned with material goods and status.[18] One study concluded that the authoritarian is so emotionally insecure in modern society that he desperately seeks definitive answers. Such answers are provided by conventional institutions such as churches, commercial groups, and recognized national leaders whose views are the same as his.[19]

It is possible to go through the Adorno-Sanford studies and find cases wherein they apply to individuals in the veterans' groups. Certainly all of the older societies officially state, not without reason, that

America must be on guard against a sinister world-wide conspiracy. In the early twenties, all organizations passed resolutions pointing out this danger, and in October, 1959, the Legion angrily re-emphasized such fears when it appeared the Cold War might have begun to thaw due to Nikita Khrushchev's American visit. Eugene Lyons wrote in the Legion's magazine that Communism was gaining in America by devious means, and he cited the reappearance of Charlie Chaplin films, the display of Soviet goods in stores, and talks between American businessmen and Soviet officials as evidence. The M.O.W.W. supported Lyons' view. Captain Joseph W. Bollenbeck wrote in the M.O.W.W. *Bulletin* that the Order had to remain alert "twelve months out of the year to nefarious plots to undermine our security." [20]

The vilification and hostility of an authoritarian nature is often expressed in the contemptuous and forceful language employed against persons who disagree with official views. The D.A.V.'s 1927 Americanism chairman, W. E. Leonard, lumped Communists, internationalists and "just plain crackpots" into one group. The Legion's California Department passed a resolution in 1955 that asked the members to "eliminate" the United Nations Educational, Scientific and Cultural Organization (UNESCO) from "American life and thought." The Legion's commission also has characterized supporters of world federalism as "wild-eyed visionaries" and "global fanatics." It stated that it wished Government workers who used the Fifth Amendment "removed from the economy" and entertained recommendations that condemned the Girl Scouts for supporting internationalism. The Legion's 1955 National Commander, Seaborn Collins, charged that the Fund for the Republic "crippled" national defense. The V.F.W., in 1953, wished to "compel" American children to study officially approved history. [21]

Seven other aspects of the Adorno-Sanford authoritarian syndrome apparently can be found among the veterans' groups. They stress the material benefits that accue from membership, and all of them express devotion to traditional middle-class virtues such as organized religion, free economic enterprise, and individualism. Definitive answers are sought in various ways. The U.S.W.V. has depended on prayer, while the M.O.W.W. discovers strength in the military training of its members. In recent years, the Legion has relied increasingly on the F.B.I.'s J. Edgar Hoover whose number two man, Lee Pennington, cooperated with Legion headquarters for several years. The Legion's magazine, in 1959, stated that softness and decay abounded in America, a view Hoover supported when he wrote in the official journal that moral training, God, the Bible, and physical punishment for delinquents would help correct the situation.[22]

Before the conclusion is reached that the older veterans' societies are completely authoritarian, the term's nature has to be scrutinized carefully and, in addition, the studies themselves must be analyzed. During the thirties, popular belief held that fascism was the accentuation of bourgeois conservatism; Gellermann and Gray implied this. Since World War II, the structure of fascism has been re-examined. Authoritarianism may run the gamut from an intense belief in law and order to reactionary radicalism. To use Hitler's Germany as an example, the Nazi state was not only far from being efficient and conservative but its policies belonged to the radical right. The Nazis never intended to preserve organized religions, the professional civil service, nor the old line officer's corps. They did their best to subvert and destroy the conventional pillars of the German state and society in a nihilistic and anarchical fashion.[23]

Technical criticism over the Adorno-Sanford studies comes from other social scientists. There is doubt as to the accuracy of the "F Scale." The measuring device fails to include any analysis of positive democratic beliefs. Another criticism is aimed at the label of authoritarian personality. Professor W. Edgar Gregory of the University of the Pacific wondered whether it might not be more accurate to say that some personalities have tendencies toward authoritarianism since personality makeup contains so many variations that categorizing such traits is dangerous.[24] There is considerable risk in trying to apply the Adorno-Sanford authoritarian studies to American veteran societies and not too much behavioral work has been done on veterans' groups alone. Usually, as in the case of Lunt and Warner's "Yankee City" series, information on veterans is incidental, so only a few qualified generalizations might be made.

The veterans' groups and their members do have a tendency to submit to strong leadership, but how blindly authoritarian their submission is cannot be precisely perceived. Apathy and ignorance condition their responses but they can be unexpectedly rebellious and vocal when factually informed and aroused. The Legion exhibits some striking examples as in 1946, when Commander John Stelle lambasted the popular Veterans Administrator, General Omar Bradley. National headquarter's staff members were upset by the attack. Justin Gray claimed that his administrative director ordered the group to support Stelle no matter what they personally felt. This the workers as a body did, although Gray said that many Legionnaires wrote letters or sent telegrams into headquarters that criticized Stelle.[25] Another incident occurred in 1955. The Legion's National Executive Committee (N.E.C.) ordered a special investigation of the UNESCO program which the Americanism Commission had long labeled subversive. The investigators discovered no subversion in UNESCO, but they did find that Legion post commanders had made extensive use of anti-UNESCO hate-mongering pamphlets written by Joseph Kamp, Henry McFarland, and C. J. McGinley. The Americanism Commission, however, protested the special investigators' report, and the N.E.C., heeding the Commission, refused to submit it to the 1955 national convention. Extreme criticism boiled up both inside and outside the Legion engulfing the N.E.C. but the committee ignored the furor and supported the Americanism Commission.[26] In the U.S.W.V.'s case it is difficult to find an orientation toward the cult of the authoritarian leader. The twentieth century has often been an era of strong, charismatic leadership in many nations, including the United States, yet, the U.S.W.V.'s *beau ideal* has remained William McKinley. Not even the vibrant Theodore Roosevelt retains the hold on the U.S.W.V. membership that McKinley does.[27]

Thus, in view of the intricacy and abstruse nature of the subject, authoritarianism possesses spectral characteristics and must retain its shade-like quality as a label describing much that is associated with the veterans' organizations. Where authoritarianism does seem to appear most palpably among the societies is in their counter subversive tactics. In 1941 the D.A.V.'s Americanism Chairman William J. McCluskey stated that civil liberties must be abridged so that ultimate freedom might survive. He suggested erection of concentration camps to house an estimated one million persons that he considered un-American. The V.F.W. and the Legion have acted in somewhat the same manner. Both maintain large file systems which they readily make available to the F.B.I., the military services, Congress, and other so-called patriotic groups. Justin Gray said in 1948, much to the subsequent indignation of Legion officials, that its files consisted of unsubstantiated gossip and that anyone who publicly disagreed with Legion policy automatically went into the subversive sections. The Legion like all the veterans' associations also has vigorously supported Congressional un-American investigations and for several years also has been the prime mover of the sixty members All-American Conference to Combat Communism which eventually hopes to affect "the destruction of all threats to Americanism." In

1953 the Legion's monthly magazine made favorable editorial reference to Republican Senator Joseph R. McCarthy, thus enjoying the peak of his power and popularity as a demagogic investigator of all that he considered un-American. Official lists of acceptable columnists and journalists have been published. Among those conservative journalists who have been favorably recommended by the Legion are Westbrook Pegler, Fulton Lewis, Jr., David Lawrence, James Burnham, William Buckley, and the late Whitaker Chambers. Articles also were written that condemned liberals including Professor Gordon Craig of Stanford, Edward J. Fitzgerald of the New York Herald Tribune, former C.B.S. commentator Edward R. Murrow, the Ford Foundation's Robert M. Hutchins, and the entire membership of the Americans for Democratic Action.[28]

The Legion has maintained training schools for counter subversion, and its Washington branch was once headed by an ex-F.B.I. agent. The Americanism Commission has claimed that demands for its specialists in counter subversion exceed the ability of the division to meet them. In past years the Legion has used such experts as Elizabeth Dilling and Harvey Matusow. In 1948, Gray charged that Elizabeth Dilling once referred to Dwight Eisenhower as ' "Ike the Kike.' " Matusow was an F.B.I. communist undercover agent who claimed that being a professional informer was "a good racket" and that ex-communists obtained lots of glamor. In 1955 he was belatedly jailed in a Federal penitentiary for perjuring himself while testifying about 244 persons he had linked with communism. The Legion, however, has never seen fit to comment on Matusow's conviction.[29]

Some liberals assume that the veterans' groups and their leaders are more intolerant than the mass of Americans. Gellermann, in 1938, contended that the Legion was fascist and he urged American society to unite against the organization. In 1948 Justin Gray resigned from the Legion because of the hierarchy's illiberalism although he claimed to have rejoined later because he knew there were liberal Legionnaires in the organization whom he hoped to attract to his standard and protest the leadership.[30]

Doubt has been cast on the liberals' assumptions by the appearance of an extensive public opinion analysis in 1955. The late Professor Samuel A. Stouffer, a Harvard sociologist, conducted a massive behavioral study of citizens in the tense spring of 1954. The research was set against the backdrop of Senator Joseph R. McCarthy's ludicrous but bitter fight with the United States Army over alleged Communists within its ranks. Stouffer wished to find the public's reaction to the issues of communism, conformism, and civil liberties. He asked 6,000 Americans two broad questions: how seriously did they regard the issue of internal subversion, and how far were they prepared to support civil liberties in regard to non-conformists.[31] The public's answers were measured against those of community leaders typified by patriotic society chiefs, newspaper publishers, mayors, and union heads. The results were startling in many respects as they showed that neither the community leaders nor the public were unduly concerned about the issues of internal subversion or the loss of civil rights. The study, moreover, found that the community leaders tended to be markedly more tolerant than the public. Patriotic chiefs were among the least tolerant in the leadership group, but even they appeared to be more so than the average citizen.[32]

The behavioral analysis included only members of the V.F.W. and the Legion among its respondents since other veterans' societies were considered too small. Stouffer concluded that veterans as a class belonged in the tolerant group in comparison to the public. Unorganized veterans, however, tended to be more liberal than members of the two largest organizations. World War II veterans generally were more flexible in thought than older veterans. The higher the degree of education, the greater the amount of tolerance he found. The two big veterans' groups apparently have a disproportionately low membership from the two educational extremes.[33] Stouffer wondered what might happen to the older organizations if young, educated, thoughtful veterans joined. He implied that there was a good chance that the ideologies and practices of the V.F.W. and the Legion might change as a result.[34]

A few criticisms and generalizations may be drawn from Stouffer's book. The sample on veterans is small and there is also a question as to the reliability of a respondent's answer. Do they indicate inmost thoughts or socially acceptable replies? Stouffer's desire that young perceptive veterans make their presence known seems unrealistic. The history of the largest group is replete with instances where dissenters have been resolutely ignored. Occasionally, as in the Stelle-Bradley affair, leaders were vigorously challenged. Stelle, however, continued his attack with N.E.C. approval. Rarely have major policies fundamentally been changed as a result of dissent. For instance, despite opposition over suppression of the UNESCO report, the Legion has continued officially to consider the program subversive.[35]

The study indicates that blanket indictments of the veterans' illiberalism must be tempered for it appears that many Americans are conceivably more intolerant than the ex-servicemen. The public is not possessed of democratic virtue because of its mass, any more than the veteran is an Americanism expert because of war service. Both liberal critics and patriotic leaders should recast their method of thinking in respect to criticism and patriotism.

The question of a correlation between the veterans and authoritarianism is a complex one. A qualified relationship exists, but to date it is not the ultimate of authoritarianism as it has been understood since World War II, although the frustrations of the Cold War may well change this. There are as many variations of authoritarianism as there are of liberalism, conservatism, and Marxism. Social psychologist Erich Fromm states that one trait of the authoritarian is his worship of the past. What has been, must eternally be. In this respect, the older veterans' societies and some of its members undoubtedly are authoritarianally inclined. They revere the past and seek to maintain the *status quo*. The use of activist measures, as well, in counter subversion programs seems to indicate a prevalent degree of authoritarianism. Often, however, it must be noted that these activities are ignored or condemned by some veterans.[36]

The problem also exists as to whether or not the veterans' organizations are unique in their approach to counter subversion. The counter-subversion programs apparently contain elements and strains of authoritarianism, but perhaps they are symptomatic of general twentieth century American society and not confined solely to the patriotic associations. This may absolve the veterans of some of the blame poured upon them by their critics, but it is hardly reassuring in a larger sense.

CHAPTER VIII

THE NEW VETERANS

There is an ambiguity in being an ex-serviceman today. Only a small percentage of those able to join veterans' groups do so, yet the veterans' class has never been so big. While all persons hope that a major war will never occur, the policy of military deterrence and the doctrine of limited warfare almost guarantees the continuance of a veterans' stratum for years to come. But under such circumstances what happens to that special patina of exclusiveness born of national service and worn by the organized veterans for so many years? Over a very short period of time it will come to pass that the person who has never served will be in the minority rather than the reverse.

The veterans' societies have long been on record as stating that they were in a better position to recognize and defend Americanism because they alone have fought for it and suffered on its behalf which, indeed, many of them certainly have done. In the age breaking about us, however, the electronic technicians, who scan scopes and assemble rockets in relative ease and safety, are free world fighters as surely as those who fought in the past or those now being shot at in some isolated foreign river valley. As for the men who will serve militarily in an old-fashioned fighting sense in this new era, there are also problems of evaluation. For example, attempts will have to be made equating duty in the peculiar and publicized 1958 Lebanese expedition with the contemporary severe trials being borne by Americans in the clandestine engagements of Southeastern Asia.

When all of these factors are considered, it is seen that the veterans' traditional role of being those who fought in a single mighty war for the preservation of the nation is altered. Being a veteran, in short, will have lost its original significance and such a change may transmute the future concept of Americanism. No one may foretell what the nature of tomorrow's veteran will be. The emergence, however, of two societies during World War II could provide significant information about contemporary trends in patriotism among a newer type of organized veteran. Their history is so short and incomplete that the task of assessing its importance must remain qualified. Their patriotic record to date shows that their nationalistic orientation may prove to represent a different notion of Americanism from that of the older groups. Whether or not this new approach or interpretation of patriotism will find general acceptance is not ascertainable but its very existence warrants inclusion in this chronicle.

*   *   *

As World War II ended, the two largest veterans' organizations vigorously recruited the ex-fighting men. At first, they were undecided about, and even suspicious of, the servicemen of the latest war. Some members of the Legion, for instance, did not want young men to come in and upset the status quo. In the end, however, the Legion by and large changed its attitude and successfully swelled its ranks for it had much to offer in size, equipment, and power. The V.F.W.'s membership jumped as well, from approximately 250,000 in 1940 to well over a million by early 1947. Paradoxically, exclusiveness played a part in the V.F.W.'s expansion, for much of its appeal lay in its overseas service requirement which also enabled it to recruit men in foreign lands. The V.F.W. earned popularity among servicemen, too, by successfully supporting terminal leave pay for enlisted personnel as well as for officers.[1]

But not all veterans wished to join the old line organizations. Some simply wanted a society open only to World War II participants; others expressed contempt of the convention-time antics of the older ex-soldiers; a few objected to the Legion's bonus raids of the thirties and its seeming illiberalism.[2] Whatever their complaints were about the existing societies, various of the new veterans began organizing throughout the country from 1943 until 1945, with many service personnel forming the nuclei of their clubs on college campuses.

One such group gathered under Gilbert A. Harrison, a University of California at Los Angeles (U.C.L.A.) graduate, who began to write service friends in January, 1943, with whom he wished to exchange views on the postwar world. The correspondents used as a regular channel of communication the office of the U.C.L.A. University Religious Conference. Generally, they possessed similar backgrounds and outlooks and, according to one of them, most were college graduates who were pacifists and isolationists during the thirties.[3]

Basic ideas emerged from the mass of exchanged letters and bulletins. The correspondents listed world peace as being easily the most important postwar issue, and they felt that the only way to guarantee it was through an effective international organization. Neither

America nor any single nation alone could guarantee peace and free-dom. Since individual nationalism threatened security and liberty, the only type of government capable of preserving democratic prin-ciples and peace was some form of world administration.[4] Other aims and goals supported this primary ideal. They were liberal in spirit and included the extension of civil liberties, equality of opportunity, and social legislation designed to mitigate poverty and disease. Behind these general aims lay the realization that America's domestic well-being depended upon the stability of the outside world. Many of the correspondents once believed in isolation, and it failed them. By 1944 the small group became internationalists.[5]

Harrison and others knew that as individuals they would have little weight. It was decided that the writers must organize and become a veterans' pressure group. Although they certainly acted as other veterans before them had in this respect, in other ways they radically departed from tradition by not seeking any material benefits such as pensions or a bonus. Instead, they tried to affect national policies through the application of moral judgments. The associates were not organization men, but history demonstrated to them that veterans' groups emerged from every war. The old-line societies tried to keep America unchanged, and Harrison's friends knew this was impossible. The new league's purpose would be to prepare America for the future.[6]

Harrison needed a discharged serviceman of liberal ideals to set up the administrative machinery. He found him in Charles G. Bolté, Dartmouth graduate and a one-legged veteran of Britain's Eighth Desert Army. Bolté traveled and wrote extensively from 1944 until 1946 and attained much publicity, as well as an invitation from Mrs. Franklin Roosevelt to the White House.[7]

The alliance of correspondents officially organized in July, 1944 as the American Veterans Committee (A.V.C.). Among those who joined were the Army's famous cartoonist Bill Mauldin, Franklin D. Roosevelt, Jr., writer E. J. Kahn, Jr., millionaire G. Mennen Williams, and magazine editor Michael Straight. By 1946 the A.V.C. was attracting favorable comment from the National Association for the Advancement of Colored People (N.A.A.C.P.) and Walter Reuther's United Auto Workers. Liberal magazines such as *The Christian Cen-tury, The Nation and The New Republic* editorially praised the organ-ization.[8]

Such endorsements, however, hardly enhanced the new group in the eyes of many. The A.V.C.'s *Bulletin* charged that not only the United States Army, and the older veterans' societies, but the American Communist Party, as well, opposed the new organization. The A.V.C. earned the Army's displeasure when Pacific chapters publicly denounced its segregation policies and claimed that the military tried to destroy the chapters. Liberal magazines, such as *The New Republic* and *The Nation*, editorially denounced the Legion and V.F.W. for harrassing the A.V.C. The magazines and the *Bulletin* stated that the older groups refused their support because the A.V.C. recruited Merchant Mariners whom the V.F.W. and Legion felt were not legitimate war veterans despite their casualties and generally because it was a too liberally obstreperous organization. The Veterans Administration, nonetheless, officially and routinely recognized the A.V.C. in September, 1946.[9] The Communists in 1944 and 1945 began the first of a series of attacks on the liberal veterans. Walter Bernstein, a New York Communist, stated that Bolté and Harrison were unrealistic since they regarded the typical veteran as a college graduate let loose in a strange immoral world. The A.V.C. lacked grass roots support and would have none as long as it refused to join the labor movement.[10]

Communist Party policy lay behind Bernstein's attack. From 1944 until 1945, the party had tried to infiltrate the Legion. The purpose was to utilize it, since it was "an integral part of American life on the community level." The special target was the Legion's non-official, hence vulnerable, National Conference of Union Labor Legionnaires composed of trade unionists. The Communists were successful and so blackened the eye of the N.C.U.L.L. that it was driven from the Legion and later disintegrated. The Communists were successful where Homer Chaillaux was a failure.[11]

In 1946 the Communists turned their attention to the A.V.C. charging that the liberals "divided the progressive reform" of the older veterans' outfits. They wished the A.V.C. members to leave that organization and join forces with them in infiltrating the V.F.W. and Legion but the A.V.C. membership refused. The acrimony which grew between the Communists and the liberals became the A.V.C.'s most serious problem between 1946 and 1948. Communists began joining the A.V.C. and successfully took over a number of chapters in the New York area. The A.V.C. knew that the infiltration posed a dilemma so in June, 1948, its Research Committee conducted a poll of its members in an effort to determine what the liberals wished to do about the Communists. A majority of the A.V.C. membership declared that they thought it was undemocratic to eject the Communists but, on the other hand, the members were extremely fearful and cognizant of the fact that if the Communists remained they might take over the A.V.C.[12]

The A.V.C.'s Communists never wavered over such democratic deliberations. Julian H. Franklin, a New York member, related in 1947 how they worked. Communists joined chapters singly at first; then others would appear in greater numbers. They were dynamic speakers and, if they obtained control of a chapter, they dispensed with parliamentary procedure explaining that it was inefficient. The A.V.C.'s national leadership also came under attack as part of the same plan. The Communists claimed that Bolté, Roosevelt, and Harrison were hypocrites because they were incipient conservatives and ruthlessly ambitious for personal gain at the expense of A.V.C.'s members.[13]

In 1948 the fight over infiltration reached its highest peak. The top A.V.C. administrative board, the National Planning Committee (N.P.C.), in September suspended the *Daily Worker's* editor, John Gates, who was an A.V.C. member. Then it revoked the heavily Communist New York Area Council's charter. The December, 1948 Cleveland national convention voted overwhelmingly to expel its Communist members and an anti-Communist platform was adopted. As a result, all new members signed a pledge stating that they were not Communists.[14]

The A.V.C.'s monthly *Bulletin* editorially admitted that the fight's aftermath almost finished the organization. Membership fell off to 50,000 and it has never regained its immediate postwar size of 75,000. But the group, battered as it was, could claim with satisfaction that it met Communism head-on and defeated it by democratic means. Years before political demagogues found it fashionable to ululate about the postwar Communist menace, the liberals already were fighting the enemy and won the match without subverting democratic ideals and principles. On this point alone the tiny A.V.C. should earn prominent mention in the social history of this period. It has, furthermore, continued to spread the gospel of democratic liberalism as a recent national platform illustrates. The policy statement applauded the 1954 Supreme Court desegregation decision since the A.V.C. has long considered the integration issue America's primary problem. The delegates also voted for Federal aid to education and public health. They resolved that United States' foreign policy should sympathetically identify itself with countries that sought escape from dictatorship or colonialism.[15]

The A.V.C.'s liberalism is in deep contrast with the official policies of the older veterans' societies. The most striking difference between them is the concept of nationalism. The A.V.C. regards extreme nationalism as a menace to world peace yet it has stated that American democratic institutions offer a beneficial life to all men. Such institutions, however, might be best guaranteed by active support of the United Nations.[16]

The A.V.C.'s views of Americanism also differ from the older groups. It never has bogged itself down trying to define 100 per cent Americanism. The closest it ever came to inaugurating an Americanism program was its annual Civil Rights Award which, the National Secretary, R. Hal Silvers, explained, was presented to any American who "makes democracy work." Among its recipients have been Adlai E. Stevenson, Mrs. Franklin Roosevelt, Dr. Ralph Bunche, Illinois Democrat Senator Paul Douglas, and Michigan's Governor G. Mennen Williams.[17]

Civil rights and civil liberties lie at the center of the A.V.C.'s Americanism. The organization has instituted law suits on behalf of minority groups and, in the realm of civil liberties, it loudly and vocally opposed the late Senator Joseph R. McCarthy while the N.P.C. called for his impeachment in 1950.[18] In these fields, the A.V.C. often has used the Legion as a whipping boy. The 1956 National Chairman, Mickey Levine, traveled through five southern states interviewing Negro veterans and found serious discrimination against them. He accused the Legion of making its local southern posts available to the White Citizens' Council. In 1958 the A.V.C. gave its Bill of Rights Award to the nine Negro students of Little Rock, Arkansas who braved white mobs to attend the first desegregated high school. In February, 1958 the A.V.C. *Bulletin* scornfully published a photograph of Arkansas' white-supremist Governor Orville Faubus receiving the Georgia Legion Department's Americanism award. The *Bulletin* pointedly observed that the Legion gave its trophy to Governor Faubus as the A.V.C. gave its award to the nine Negro children.[19] Levine asked Congress to investigate the Legion in September, 1959. He said that the government should withdraw the Legion's tax-exempt status unless it desegregated its elite Forty and Eight Society. Congress took no action.[20]

It is difficult to judge the effects of the A.V.C.'s liberal Americanism views. Its actions are the antitheses of those policies followed by the older groups, but the liberals' main value as organized patriots lies in their articulateness. Such skills are lost, however, without media outlet and, in this respect, the A.V.C. is stymied. In recent years, the only journals that have carried A.V.C. events have been liberal ones. The group seems only to reach an audience it does not have to convince.[21]

The A.V.C.'s sociological background also appears to limit its appeal. In 1954 Columbia University conducted a behavioral survey of the group. According to the statistics, the average member was a college graduate in his thirties. He earned over $7,000 a year and owned his own house and appliances. Politically, he considered himself a liberal and a majority rated Franklin D. Roosevelt and Adlai E. Stevenson over Dwight D. Eisenhower. His magazine preferences in order were: *The New Yorker, Time, Life,* and *The New Republic.* The Columbia study listed the *Ladies Home Journal, The Reader's Digest, Life,* and *McCall's* as national preferences.[22]

The A.V.C. creates an impression of being Professor Stouffer's idealized veterans' society. The truth, however, is that its voice, though loud for its size, is often unheeded. Many members of Congress joined the A.V.C., such as Representative James Roosevelt, Senator Paul Douglas, and Oregon's Democratic Senator, the late Richard Neuburger. Despite, or because of, such Congressional support, it has never been chartered by Congress. The principal A.V.C. strength has been its ability to keep an eye on other veterans' groups, and it has offered an organization to those persons not satisfied with the larger ones' official anouncements or actions. Unlike a sister association, also founded in 1944, however, the A.V.C.'s social base is not broad enough and thus it has not been able to speak for all the veterans of World War II.[23]

The outfit that stands the best chance of representing the Second World War's veterans is the American Veterans of World War II (Amvets). Its history has been tame compared to the A.V.C.'s. At its inception, unlike the liberal group, it did not establish high moral goals or principles. Originally, its members simply wanted a World War II fraternal association.[24] The Amvets' early policies seemed irresolute and Jack Hardy, 1945 National Commander, was representative in this sense. He admitted that he wished to avoid a public stand on any problem and hoped the organization would follow a middle course. The lack of leadership hurt the society. A 1946 editorial in its *National Bulletin* stated that the group was about to founder due to organizational aimlessness and lack of money.[25] In one area, however, the Amvets did not vacillate. Its U.N. policy paralleled the A.V.C.'s. In 1950 accompanied by the liberals, it joined the World Veterans Federation. In addition to its support of internationalism, Amvets backed the UNESCO program within the United States.[26]

In the realm of Americanism Amvets originally started to emulate the Legion. From 1947 to 1949 a few national headquarters officials started counter-subversion activities against alleged Communists who usually were people critical of the Amvets. In 1947 Executive Director Allen P. Solada demanded that the University of Missouri investigate its student newspaper because the students criticized the group for baiting Communists. Solada announced that he was on a crusade to suppress any attacks on the organization. National Commander Ed Corry continued in much the same spirit when, in 1948, he told the House Un-American Affairs Committee that all American Communists should be emasculated politically and economically.[27]

In 1949 changes began to occur within the group. *The A.V.C. Bulletin* commented editorially that a hint of liberalism had appeared in Amvets' policies. There was even talk of a merger between the two newest societies, but the A.V.C. turned the proposal down because, according to the N.P.C., Amvets wished to raid the Federal Treasury for benefits—a policy that disgusted the A.V.C.[28] By 1950 Amvets' first seemingly liberal commander, Harold Russell, took office, a post he has held off and on for the better part of a decade. Russell is a double amputee who received fame as the disabled sailor in the Academy Award film, "The Best Years of Our lives." As National Commander, he has led his group toward more idealistic policies. The Communist-hunting tactics of Solada and Corry have been dropped; the organization, unlike the Legion, gave vigorous support to President Truman's conduct of the Korean conflict; and it also appointed a committee to see if the Army's desegregation policies were being carried out and which found that the Army had done well in that field.[29] The new leadership has revived the Amvets' fortunes. Membership approached 125,000 in 1954, according to *Collier's*. The magazine editorially stated that the group was the largest and most successful of all the World War II veterans' societies noting that, unlike the Legion, there appeared to be no king-makers in the organization.[30]

The Amvets is the most representative veterans' association to emerge from World War II. In structure, it resembles the older outfits. Like the others, its officers bear semi-military titles, there is a female auxiliary, and an elite fun-making group called the "Sad Sacks." Warner's and Lunt's sociological studies indicate that groups cast in such a pattern are composed predominately of the middle and lower middle classes. No behavioral survey of the Amvets has been conducted but its size and social activities seem to give it a broader base than the A.V.C.[31]

The Amvets' biggest departure from the old-line groups has been in its Americanism program. In 1954 Martin D. Schwartz, Chairman of the Americanism Committee, decided that the concept of Americanism needed re-evaluation since patriotic groups tended to appropriate the word for narrow ends. Amvets obtained an unencumbered grant of $25,000 from the Ford Foundation to study Americanism and base a program upon the study's results.[32]

The program first appeared in 1959. It is remarkable in its contrast to the ones of the older societies, for it contains no pat definition of Americanism, and the Americanism Committee, moreover, claims that veterans hold no monopoly on patriotism. The program's basis is educational and revolves around group discussions. Discussion leaders are trained in group dynamics and are provided with topics by the national headquarters where material is not written by headquarters' personnel. Usually, the information consists of books and monographs written by nationally known scholars, among whom are Richard Hofstadter, Arthur M. Schlesinger, Jr., Robert E. Cushman, Carl Van Doren, Richard Heffner, and James G. Randall.[33] The Committee tries to avoid stressing an official viewpoint, and discussion leaders are cautioned not to inject official or personal opinions into the talks. The program's directors discovered that almost all the meetings culminated in a discussion of current topics for which they have made allowances by incorporating contemporary subjects into the program. Under this plan, an analysis of Thomas Jefferson, for instance, is correlated with a study of the separation of church and state, since the Committee has found that most group participants do not realize that many seemingly modern issues have been faced by earlier generations of Americans.[34]

The Committee has made no expansive claims as to the program's effectiveness, announcing in 1957 that the discussions had met with but varying degrees of success. The consensus, however, was that it should be continued. The Washington, D.C. national headquarters eventually expects to train about 120 group leaders but the program, as of 1957, was considered still to be in the formative stage and immediate results were not then anticipated.[35]

In one respect the Amvets program is suspiciously like the older societies' activities. Admitting that the Committee's motivation was not purely altruistic, Chairman Schwartz stated in 1957 that it wished to make a significant contribution to the United States but that its collateral benefits (meaning effect on prestige and membership) were too important to be ignored.[36] Although the Amvets' Americanism activities have been unlike those employed by the V.F.W. and the Legion, its utilitarian or commercial aspect has dimmed its nobility of purpose. The A.V.C. seems to be the only veterans' society that does not put a material evaluation on its Americanism. The Amvets, on the other hand, are more to be complimented than condemned. It stood every chance of becoming an imitation American Legion but it did not do so, and its Americanism program is a step in an enlightened direction. There is a danger to the Amvets' liberalism, however, for no one has ascertained what would happen if its present leadership is displaced. The Americanism program would suffer if new leaders could not resist the temptation to use it for recruitment and publicity. Schwartz' 1957 admission showed how easily such a process might occur.

The most heartening news in regard to the A.V.C. and the Amvets is their seeming capacity to remain flexible. World War II's veterans are no longer young men, yet the A.V.C. has maintained its vigor and idealism. Its numbers are small, but its record demonstrates that the membership will fight for its collective ideals with terrier-like tenacity. The Amvets, too, appear to have shown open-mindedness. Significantly, its liberalism appeared just as America entered an era of anti-Communist hysteria.[37]

Their combined ranks are minuscule compared to the other veterans' organizations. As the two associations face the future, however, they both realistically acknowledge America's problems in domestic and foreign affairs. Neither has tried to ignore them under the cloak of the Communist issue, the delusion of affluence, or the desire for special benefits. The Amvets even has tempered its pension philosophy as it wishes to have only legitimate compensation for the disabled veteran, widows, and orphans. Composed largely of World War II and Korean veterans, the two societies' past has been meaningful. Despite limited size, their future might be significant if the present spirit should persist.[38]

CHAPTER IX

CONCLUSION

With nostalgic fondness, many Americans look back upon the decade and a half before the country entered World War I. Then, it is alleged, truly existed the good old days when the nation was composed of a society that was uncomplicated and peacefully harmonious. No one believes in this fanciful image with more resoluteness than the organized veterans' groups founded before World War II, but, in actuality, things were often quite the opposite from what they now seem. The William McKinley-Theodore Roosevelt America of sentimental memory never really existed in precisely the form later generations wish to believe it did, for by 1900 urban-industrialization and the rise of a mass society already was reshaping America into a powerfully disturbing new form. Coincidental with this phenomenon was the country's emergence from its self-created sense of isolation and American life, as a result, was irreparably transformed. The twentieth century American scene continued to present a chaotic picture with population shifts also adding instability to the ever-changing nation. Increasingly, the so-called average American was turned from an individualistic rural resident into a city dweller dependent upon an industrial society. He also tended to be mercilessly subject to social, economic and psychological forces beyond his comprehension and ability to manage. Seemingly, old traditions were no longer controlling factors as American civilization was becoming far too fluid for them to exercise any sense of direction. Industrialism created different types of jobs and classes and with the new society came a multiplicity of loyalties based on economic, religious and racial ties. To some persons, the country was in such a state of serious turmoil that order could only come if all of the innumerable loyalties were synthesized into a single national spirit of Americanism.

There was a role to be played in this synthesis by social and service organizations which might strengthen a feeling of national loyalty in serving as a tie between their individual members and the mystique of Americanism. The societies furnished security and stability to their adherents. In such circumstances personal happiness was achieved

112

by the membership, whose sense of private satisfaction, in turn, was reflected in their professed love of the nation.[1]

From 1898 until the mid-century, one type of group that has tried to link the symbols of nationalism and the individual together has been the veterans' society. The ex-servicemen, like most persons, often reacted on the nation's behalf in response to the organizations with which they identified themselves. Consequently, the members felt that what was good for the veterans' associations was good for the country. Such actions by the veterans often were undertaken in the sincere belief that their views represented the true spirit of Americanism.

As the century progressed, the organized veterans' concepts of Americanism also changed. Americanism is, in essence, loyalty and the societies founded between the Spanish-American War and the early twenties generaly held one view of it, while those created after 1941 adhered to another. Basically, the older organizations' concept was unsophisticated, or even provincial. The traditional veterans' groups tried to give Americanism a fixed content and they predicted their theory of it on the view that the societies' state of flux was always dangerous for the nation. They attempted to dissolve or transmute the myriad of sub-loyalties among American citizens, not believing that multistrand allegiances might strengthen the national spirit. In short, the older veterans' groups officially demanded a more direct form of loyalty.[2]

In practice, this direct loyalty was to be given to an idealized image of America, a nation where the national heritage had to be preserved, change rejected, and the *status quo* defended. The veterans officially insisted upon uncritical acceptance of the country as an already finished product while the values of middle-class America were held as inviolate. Thus, the nation's economic, social and political institutions were felt to be perfect and complete. Each succeeding generation of veterans expressed the spirit of Americanism in slightly different ways, and naturally, every manifestation reflected the problems and experiences peculiar to that era.

U.S.W.V. spokesmen emotionally never have left the period from 1898 to 1906. Events during the twentieth century have poured in upon the membership buffeting them about severely and, consequently, they long for the country to stay as they imagine it was at McKinley's death. To them, a man's faith in America has been equated with his religion and war service and their spirit of Americanism is more personalized than that of their successors. Other veterans' societies might proclaim the same beliefs but the veterans of 1898 represent a more sentimental and individualistic age. The ritual of Americanism is meticulously observed by them; however, its practice is simple and strikingly fundamentalist in comparison to a later generation's.

The Spanish War veterans' spirit of Americanism has been intense, and its tenor is romantically martial, but seldom has it been used as a club to bludgeon non-believers. Although like most of the societies, they have exploited their patriotism for welfare benefits, the heroes of ninety-eight resisted efforts to organize and mobilize their spirit of Americanism. In 1957 while at Little Rock, Arkansas, whose racial problems symbolically erupted around the aged veterans, the U.S.-W.V.'s Chaplain-in-Chief Charles M. Charlton summed up the dwindling society's Americanism:

Life, liberty, property, character, reputation, and veracity are something that no man has a right to take from another man. Inclusive recognition of the infinite and eternal values arising from man's relation to his God. [sic] For man, regardless, is God's expression of himself. [sic] Our generation, the men of 1898, believe in that kind of Americanism.[3]

World War I affected the ex-servicemen's spirit of Americanism more than any event of the century. Prior to 1917, one aspect of Americanism was the removal of the hyphen. The problems of assimilation attendant to the new immigration helped engender tensions among many citizens and wartime emotionalism inevitably created further suspicion against anything foreign. As a natural consequence, it became patriotic to voice such fears and in some cases, Americanism became harsh with antagonism. Critics of the American scene thought that it even appeared authoritarian as, at times, various leaders of the World War I societies subscribed to such practices.

The largest of the World War I associations was the American Legion. It borrowed its Americanism phraseology and philosophy from Theodore Roosevelt, whose wartime Americanism was not immune from the passions of the time. The veterans of 1917, however, found war emotionalism hard to sustain. They drew upon new techniques of organizational management to help maintain and promulgate their spirit of Americanism since the First World War's mobilization effort had illustrated the advantages of such organization. With marked efficiency, activities could be centrally directed and pressure applied at critical times. This technique was wedded to war-induced chauvinism and the amalgamation was the Legion's major innovation in their field of patriotism.

From a pragmatic point of view, the Legion's Americanism has been successful, and other societies gratefully have copied various parts of its program. Advertising, sales promotion, and public relations have been inseparable from the Legion's and V.F.W.'s patriotic programs as the tired passions emanating from 1919 have been kept alive for utilitarian purposes. The spirit of Americanism, in part, has become heavily tinged with commercialism. It might be argued, however, that the two organizations have had little choice but to adopt this type of Americanism. They, as well as many citizens have had difficulty in defining the term. The Legion and the V.F.W. chose to create practical, tangible programs in place of an abstraction.

The Americanism of the World War I organizations has been well received by the populace. Posts materially have aided communities and provide fellowship through social activities. No proof exists, however, that the public has accepted official policies because of local activities. Few citizens or members of the societies knew the nature of official headquarters' views and, because of the hierarchies' corporate isolation, plans apparently have been conceived in ignorance of the brotherhood's wishes. Through adroit use of public relations techniques, though, the older veterans' associations have tried to convince many that they speak for a cohesive veterans' bloc.

Despite the general acceptance of the veterans' Americanism, World War II produced some reaction against it. The newest group of veterans apparently is better educated than their elders and many young men of the forties indicated their disenchantment with the traditional societies. A vast majority never bothered to join any organization. Most of those who did join chose the old groups, but it is doubtful that they did so because of patriotism. It is more likely that they joined because the entrenched organizations provided expansive physical plants for social and recreational activities and they also knew their way along the Washington legislative paths. Membership and influence, however, declined in urban areas as the postwar era ebbed, although correspondingly it has remained high in rural sections of the country, factors which may account for the conservatism of their policies. The newest recruits, in any case, have not greatly affected official views and the older societies' spirit of Americanism continues much as it has since 1919.*

A tiny minority of World War II veterans organized separately and vigorously objected to their elders' concept of Americanism. Generally, the younger ex-servicemen have evaluated American nationalism differently from the old-line organizations which have refused to surrender much national sovereignty to a world government ideal. The

latter have stated that the United Nations existed as an instrument of
United States foreign policy and not its cornerstone. The A.V.C. and
the Amvets say by contrast, that America alone is no longer able to
guarantee its own institutions. The preservation of the American
heritage ultimately has to lie in a United Nations strongly backed by
the United States.

This divergence of belief has created a new tone in the spirit of
Americanism. The younger veterans have tried to remove its commercialized, martial aspect and they refuse to define Americanism in
exact terms. The A.V.C. says that it is an uncompromising promul-
gation of civil liberties while Amvets states that it is devotion to the
ideals of freedom for all mankind. Both associations regard it as a
positive attitude.

The older veterans have often used the spirit of Americanism in a
negative fashion and they allow little official dissent from conventional
views within or without the organizations. The younger societies try
to avoid such practices. The A.V.C.'s officials cannot act unless
the entire membership votes on policy. When the Communists were
expelled even the Marxists were given a hearing and allowed to vote
themselves. The Amvets is more centralized. Although it rules by
convention resolutions, its leaders often have taken the initiative in
formulating policy as exemplified by its Americanism program which
was a headquarters' creation. The fact that one man, such as Harold
Russell, was able to liberalize its policies showed centralized administrative control. Amvets, however, have conducted periodic polls of its
members to ascertain their sentiments and help guide policy. Generally, the surveys have been followed and it bases its U.N. suport on
such a sampling.[5]

The newer veterans have tried to remove the militancy from their
spirit of Americanism. They believe that excessive belligerency in
the nuclear age can destroy all men, a stand to which the older societies
sarcastically have responded that such a view is soft, visionary, and
unrealistic. In practice, however, the younger veterans' spirit of
Americanism is more realistic than their elders have realized. The
Amvets and the A.V.C. have never attempted to gloss over or hide the
problems facing America, whereas the older groups sometimes have
appeared confused over the United States' role in the world. Their
uncertainty and intellectual disarray have underscored the seeming
bellicosity of their Americanism while also making many aspects of
their patriotic programs inept.

The contrasts, in these respects, between the traditional societies and the younger associations are striking. The newer organizations have stated that desegregation, automation, and an expanding population are domestic problems that demand immediate attention. In foreign affairs, they stand for controlled disarmament, some form of free world government, and sympathetic support for Afro-Asian nationalism.

The older organizations' policies have been and continue to be paradoxical, for although they utilize mass propaganda skills and public relations technique, they apparently do not fully comprehend contemporary American society. Their fear of change and insistence upon conformism prevents any deep analysis of our culture or its problems. Their ruling cliques sometimes have ignored reality because it would force new interpretations of long held psychologically satisfying beliefs and preconceived ideas. The M.O.W.W.'s *Bulletin*, in 1958, provided an example of such an attitude. A year after the Sputniks went aloft its counter-intelligence section heard the Army's head of Research and Development, Lt.-General Arthur D. Trudeau, still attribute Soviet rocket successes to espionage and not to the skill of the Russian scientists. The Legion's 1955 UNESCO investigation also is illustrative in much the same fashion, for the Americanism Commission has invested too much in the way of work and prestige and is too firmly committed to have its anti-UNESCO stand officially reversed.[5] In that particular case, the outcome has disgusted many persons but it is neither a sinister nor an evil act on the Legion's part. It is simply fumbling and unimaginative, bearing out Professor Truman's contention that corporate leadership often becames distant and loses touch with practicality as well as reality.[6]

Other examples of official obtuseness lie in the employment, manipulation and utilization of traditional symbols. The old-line outfits have used conventional imagery without evaluation of its relevance to contemporary American life. The phrases "economic competition" and "rugged individualism" have been sanctified in the dogma of Americanism, yet, an American historian, David Potter of Stanford, illustrates that competition and social mobility have created a fluid and tense society. In the loneliness and fear manifest in such a society, men crave certitudes. The veterans' leagues are, in part, protective associations and it is ironic that the search for verities has often promoted an ideal which, in practice, intensifies the very insecurity and change they most fear. Nonetheless, the older groups' views and pronouncements have continued to receive vast publicity inevitably due perhaps to their very size and traditional community acceptance as well as to the general tenor of the times. The strains and anxieties brought forth by the prolonged Cold War have invariably dramatized the activities of the self-confessed patriots. Such a friction of forces, however, has created heat and energy but little light in regard to the question of loyalty.[7]

For sixty years the elder societies have wrestled with the abstraction of Americanism but by mid-century, there is still doubt concerning its meaning. As if to erase that uncertainty, most of the organizations have created diverse programs of Americanism many of whose projects have been beneficial, and some superficial, even if practical. Often the Americanism plans have blundered down blind paths while the goal of Americanism remains nebulous; the word being mistaken for the deed, and the gesture for the principle. In this context patriotism means only a passionate repressiveness leading to stultifying conformism.

By accepting the inconsistencies of American and international life, however, one small segment among the younger veterans have indicated that the spirit of Americanism has changed. They prefer the turmoil of democratic national loyalty to a more direct, rigid allegiance to the nation. They realize that national loyalty is built upon subloyalties to primary groups and that America's complexity is her strength. There should be no single standard of Americanism in such a pluralistic society for diversity of opinion and the clash of ideals are the hallmarks of a democratic social order.

The veterans' spirit of Americanism has changed from the days of 1898 and 1917. In those eras, the spirit reflected the unease and provincialism of the ex-servicemen. The new veterans appear to be more certain of themselves and of the nation. Their strongly reflected spirit of Americanism shows signs of a maturity which could augur well for the nation in the days to come. Despite their small numbers it is necessary that they be heard, for America will have terrible need of their sober good sense. The resurgence of radical right-wing societies at home, and the intensified pressures of Communism against the Free World abroad demands that the newest generation of veterans exercise their responsible American spiritualism and thus make it viable. The alternative might well be a tragedy for the American democratic ideal.

REFERENCES

CHAPTER I

1. Easily the two best books about nineteenth-century veterans are Mary R. Dearing's detailed and charmingly written *Veterans in Politics; The Story of the G.A.R.* (Baton Rouge, 1952), and Wallace Evans Davies' comprehensive *Patriotism on Parade; The Story of Veterans' and Hereditary Organizations in America, 1783-1900* (Cambridge, Massachusetts, 1955). About the only two twentieth-century veterans' groups that have been examined have been the American Legion and the American Veterans Committee. For the former see Roscoe Baker's well-written and specialized account, *The American Legion and American Foreign Policy* (New York, 1954); Marcus Duffield's anti-Legion, *King Legion* (New York, 1931); William Gellerman's unfriendy, pioneering sociological analysis, *The American Legion as Educator* (New York, 1938); Justin Gray's exposé of the Legion's Americanism Commission, *The Inside Story of the Legion* (New York, 1948); Marquis James' fascinating and one-sided pro-Legion history of its earliest years, *A History of the American Legion* (New York, 1923); Richard S. Jones' later semi-official *History of the American Legion* (New York, 1946); Richard Waller's fair-minded *The Veteran Comes Back* (New York, 1944); and George S. Wheat's perfervid, uncritical account of the Legion's founding, *The Story of the American Legion* (New York, 1919). The best book on the American Veterans Committee is by one of its founders, Charles Bolte, *The New Veteran* (New York, 1945). Bolte is a sensitive and perceptive observer of the changes in the new breed of veteran. Unfortunately, there is nothing comparable on the American Veterans of World War II and Korea unless it is Harold Russell and Victor Rosey, *Victory in My Hands* (New York, 1949), an account of Harold Russell's life which included being one of the leaders of the American Veterans of World War II and Korea. The story is important, but this account is superficial.

2. For the Revolutionary period see Stanford University's John C. Miller, *Triumph of Freedom, 1775-1783* (Boston, 1948); and Howard H. Peckham, *The War for Independence; A Military History* (Chicago, 1958). The War of 1812 and Manifest Destiny are analyzed in Francis F. Beirne, *The War of 1812* (New York, 1949); George Dangerfield, *The Era of Good Feelings* (New York, 1952); and Bernard De Voto, *Year of Decision, 1846* (Boston, 1940).

3. Perhaps the best historian writing today on nationalism is Hans Kohn, professor of history at The City College of New York; see Hans Kohn, *The Idea of Nationalism; A Study in Its Origins and Background* (New York, 1944); *The Mind of Germany; The Education of a Nation* (New York, 1960); and *American Nationalism; An Interpretive Essay* (New York, 1957); also, Boyd C. Shafer, *Nationalism: Myth or Reality* (New York, 1955).

4. It has been generally underemphasized by recent historians that Bancroft, Parkman, William Hickling Prescott, and John Lothrop Motley enunciated the thesis of Teutonic cultural superiority without the aid of evolutionary theory a whole generation before John Fiske, John W. Burgess, Theodore Roosevelt, and Albert J. Beveridge, all conditioned by Social Darwinism, picked it up again during the 1890's.

119

For an excellent appraisal of the earlier historians and their concerns with an America which they felt stemmed from Protestant North Europe, see Stanford University's David Levin, *History as Romantic Art* (Stanford, 1959).

5. Kohn, *The Idea of Nationalism; infra*, pp. 8-9.

6. For Calhoun, see Margaret L. Coit, *John C. Calhoun, Nationalist* (Boston, 1950); for Webster, see Richard N. Current, *Daniel Webster and the Rise of National Conservatism* (Boston, 1955); the character of Southern nationalism and the Civil War are found in two books by Avery O. Craven, *The Coming of the Civil War* (New York, 1957), and *The Growth of Southern Nationalism, 1848-1861* (Baton Rouge, 1953).

7. For the subject of the veterans and the immigrant, *see infra*, pp. 55-58, 75-89; for a historical analysis of Social Darwinism, see Richard Hofstadter, *Social Darwinism in American Thought* (Boston, 1955); for Germany, see Kohn, *The Mind of Germany*.

8. Hofstadter, *Social Darwinism*, pp. 170-200; for interpretations of nineteenth-century American nativism, see John Higham, *Strangers in the Land; Patterns of American Nativism* (New Brunswick, 1955), and Ray A. Billington, *The Protestant Crusade, 1800-1860; A Study of the Origins of American Nativism* (New York, 1938); for the Negro, see James B. Sellers, *Slavery in Alabama* (University of Alabama, 1950), and C. Vann Woodward, *The Strange Career of Jim Crow* (New York, 1957); the sad story of the Indians may be found in Grant Foreman's series, *Indian Removal; The Emigration of the Five Civilized Tribes of Indians* (Norman, Oklahoma, 1953), *Advancing Frontier, 1835-1860* (Norman, Oklahoma, 1933), and *Last Great Trek of the Indians* (Chicago, 1946).

9. Hofstadter, *Social Darwinism*, pp. 172-180; Albert J. Beveridge, *The Meaning of the Times* (Indianapolis, 1908), pp. 47-57; also Foster Rae Dulles, *America in the Pacific; A Century of Expansion* (New York, 1932).

10. A series of excellent books on interpreting the career and character of the colorful first Roosevelt have appeared recently, among them John M. Blum, *The Republican Roosevelt* (Cambridge, 1954), and William Henry Harbaugh, *Power and Responsibility; The Life and Times of Theodore Roosevelt* (New York, 1961); see also *infra*, pp. 18-22, 55-56, for Roosevelt's views and concern on civil liberties, race, and immigration; also Richard Hofstadter, *The American Political Tradition and the Men Who Made It* (New York, 1957), pp. 206- 237.

11. *Ibid.; infra*, p. 31.

12. Technical changes in warfare may be found in Major-General J. F. C. Fuller, *The Conduct of War, 1789-1961; A Study of the Impact of the French, Industrial, and Russian Revolutions on War and Its Conduct* (New Brunswick, 1961), and George Steele and Paul Kircher, *The Crisis We Face; Automation and the Cold War* (New York, 1960).

13. Harry Hansen (ed.)., *The 1960 World Almanac; A Book of Facts* (New York, 1960), p. 745.

14. One of the best analyses of group behavior and patriotism is found in Morton Grodzins, *The Loyal and the Disloyal; Social Boundaries of Patriotism and Treason* (Chicago, 1956); also Kohn, *American Nationalism*, and Shafer, *Nationalism: Myth or Reality*.

CHAPTER II

1. For a good, but satiric view of the war, see Walter Millis, *The Martial Spirit; A Study of Our War with Spain* (New York, 1931), pp. 219-220, 254, 320, 400-401. A more recent account is Frank Freidel's *Splendid Little War* (Boston, 1958), pp.

3-10, 33, 34-40, 61, 63, 99-100. A contemporary view emphasizing the war's rigors and aura of moral jingoism is Charles Johnson Post's *The Little War of Private Post* (Boston, 1960), pp. 3-7, 19-33, 225-300. J. A. Hobson's *Imperialism* (London, rev. ed., 1938), pp. v-xxii and Charles A. Beard's *The Idea of National Interest* (New York, 1934), pp. 65-83 blame the business community. For an evaluation of the press's role, Joseph E. Wisan, *The Cuban Crisis as Reflected in the New York Press, 1895-1898* (New York, 1934), pp. 173-200. For an analysis of imperial sentiment, see Richard Hofstadter, *Social Darwinism in American Thought* (Boston, rev. ed., 1955), pp. 170-200. John D. Hicks, *The Populist Revolt; A History of the Farmer's Alliance and the People's Party* (Minneapolis, 1931). William E. Leuchtenburg, "Progressivism and Imperialism, 1898-1916," *The Mississippi Valley Historical Review*, XXXXIX (1952), 483-504. Critiques of the American proclivity of viewing international affairs in moral terms are in George F. Kennan's *American Diplomacy, 1900-1950* (Chicago, 1950), pp. 4-20, 21-54; George E. Mowry, *The Era of Theodore Roosevelt* (New York, 1958), pp. 1-105.

2. Freidel, *Splendid Little War*, pp. 3-5, 33, 40, 61, 99, and Post, *Little War*, pp. 3-7. Bryan's pacifist sentiments prior to the war are expressed in William Jennings Bryan, *The Memoirs of William Jennings Bryan and His Wife, Mary Baird Bryan* (Philadelphia, 1925), pp. 119-120, 272-283; Paxton Hibben, *The Peerless Leader* (New York, 1929), pp. 214, 216-217, 218-223; William Jennings Bryan, *The Speeches of William Jennings Bryan, Revised and Arranged by Himself* (New York, 1909), II, 385-386, and Wayne C. Williams, *William Jennings Bryan* (New York, 1936), pp. 207-211. For works on Roosevelt, John M. Blum, *The Republican Roosevelt* (Cambridge, 1954); George E. Mowry, *Theodore Roosevelt and the Progressive Movement* (Madison, Wisconsin, 1946); Henry F. Pringle, *Theodore Roosevelt, A Biography* (New York, 1931). Julius W. Pratt, *America's Colonial Experiment* (New York, 150) pp. 1-79 analyzes "manifest destiny" in American foreign policy.

3. For war mobilization and its problems, see Franklin F. Hollbrook, ed., *Minnesota in the Spanish American War and the Philippine Insurrection*, I (Minnesota War Records Commission, St. Paul, 1923), 16-31; *New York State Historian's Report*, No. 68 (Albany, New York, April 18, 1903), pp. 9-318; Millis, *Martial Spirit*, pp. 4, 151-160, 211-220. Accounts of combat, hardship and postwar problems are in Post, *Little War*, pp. 4, 117-340; J. B. Derden to author, October 15, 1959, letter from National Adjutant of the United Spanish War Veterans.

4. Arthur M. Schlesinger, "Biography of a Nation of Joiners," *The American Historical Review*, L (1944), 1-25. Mary R. Dearing, *Veterans in Politics; The Story of the G.A.R.* (Baton Rouge, 1952), pp. 128, 230-231, 285, 305, 367-368, 379-380, 392-395, 401, 428, 430-471. See also Wallace Evans Davies, *Patriotism on Parade; The Story of Veterans' and Hereditary Organizations in America, 1783-1900* (Cambridge, Massachusetts, 1955), p. 29.

5. Captain J. Walter Mitchell, "The Spanish War Veterans," *Munsey's Magazine*, XXIX (1903), 676-678; The National Americanism Commission of the Veterans of the Foreign Wars of the United States, *The V.F.W. Story* (Kansas City, Missouri, 1959), p. 1. (Hereafter cited as V.F.W. Americanism Commission, *The V.F.W. Story*); J. B. Derden to author, October 15, 1959, letter from the National Adjutant of the United Spanish War Veterans (U.S.W.V.).

6. The United Spanish War Veterans were never loath to admit that they used the G.A.R. as an organizational model. See *House Documents*, 68 Cong., 2 sess., No. 522,

pp. 281-282. For the G.A.R.'s urban strength, see Dearing, *Veterans in Politics*, pp. 84-115.

7. Richard Hofstadter, *The Age of Reform from Bryan to F.D.R.* (New York, 1955), pp. 170, 215-216, 217-218, 224-226, 272-273, and George E. Mowry, *The California Progressives* (Berkeley, California, 1951), pp. 87-104.

8. Anthropologist Margaret Mead contended that membership in a patriotic society engendered "very real security"; Margaret Mead, *And Keep Your Powder Dry; An Anthropologist Looks at America* (New York, 1942), p. 42.

9. W. Lloyd Warner and Paul S. Lunt, *The Social Life of a Modern Community* (New Haven, 1941), I, 116. For the author's analysis of the American Legion, see below, pp. 29-41, 54-120.

10. Examples of the Spanish veterans' sustained sentiment in the face of age and little money are contained in *House Documents*, 85 Cong., 2 sess., No. 367, pp. 71-78, 82-84, 177-178, 186. The occasion was the U.S.W.V.'s 1957 convention at Little Rock, Arkansas. For examples of the U.S.W.V.'s veneration of its dead, see National Commandary, United Spanish War Veterans, *Constitution* and *By-laws* (Washington, D.C., 1905), pp. 13-18. (Hereafter cited as U.S.W.V., *Constitution*).

11. Mitchell, *loc. cit.*, pp. 676-678.

12. *Ibid.*

13. *Ibid.*; *New York Times*, September 10, 1899, 9:4. The *Times* spelled Blount's name Blunt [*sic*] and had his rank reduced to that of Lieutenant. Immunes were troops who had already had Yellow fever. Many southern negroes had the disease prior to entering the military.

14. Francis B. Simkins, *Pitchfork Ben Tillman, South Carolinian* (Baton Rouge, 1944), pp. 185-191, 380-385. The word "fully" might be declared a euphemism by Simkins. James Tillman represented the worst of "Tillmanism." He was a drinker, a demagog, who outdid his uncle in negro-baiting. During the war with Spain he was almost court-martialed for insulting a superior officer and ordering two negro soldiers flogged. In 1903, he was defeated for the governorship of South Carolina and, in cold blood, killed the newspaper editor whom he blamed for his defeat. So great was Senator Tillman's power that James was acquitted. Yet, the *New York Times* said that, in his speech on Blount's behalf, Tillman eulogized the Negro soldier; *New York Times*, September 10, 1899, 9:4.

15. Simkins, *Pitchfork Ben Tillman*, p. 383; Mitchell, *loc. cit.*, p. 677; J. B. Derden to author, October 15, 1959, letter from the National Adjutant of the U.S.W.V. Negroes seemed not to have joined the U.S.W.V., but it allowed into full membership any "native" officers or enlisted men who served honorably in the Philippine scouts; U.S.W.V., *Constitution*, pp. 19-20.

16. Mitchell, *loc. cit.*, pp. 676-678; Roosevelt actually became the first national commander of an affiliate of the U.S.W.V. The affiliate was known as the Naval and Military Order of the Spanish-American War. It was restricted to former officers only, or else enlisted men who were commissioned from the ranks. Its purpose was "more fraternal" than the U.S.W.V. It remained something of an elite within the larger U.S.W.V. Their annual conventions were held jointly; Rear Admiral Leo W. Hesselman and Major Walter M. Baker, *Historical Sketch of the Naval and Military Order of the Spanish-American War* (St. Petersburg, Florida, 1959), pp. 5-7, 17. (Hereafter cited as Hesselman and Baker, *Historical Sketch*).

17. Mitchell, *loc. cit.*, pp. 677-678; see also, the annual proceedings of the U.S.W.V. conventions. Every convention made nostalgic and lachrymose reference to McKinley. For the G.A.R.'s affection and veneration of Lincoln, see Dearing, *Veterans in Politics*,

pp. 15-117, 360-361; *House Documents*, 68 Cong., 2 sess., No. 522, p. 280. In 1924, it was decided by the U.S.W.V. that it should place flowers annually on McKinley's grave.

18. Mitchell, *loc. cit.*, pp. 676-678. Mitchell's figures appeared optimistic. No truly reliable membership figures were available until 1924. In that year the United Spanish War Veterans reported a membership of 60,000. They constituted about 26 or 27 per cent of the Spanish American War servicemen; *House Documents*, 68 Cong., 2 sess., No. 522, p. 104. By 1957, the U.S.W.V.'s membership stood at slightly over 29,000; *ibid.*, 85 Cong., 2 sess., No 367, p. 177.

19. J. B. Derden to the author, October 15, 1959, letter from the National Adjutant of the U.S.W.V. Records of the smaller societies were almost nonexistent. Any information about them came through the U.S.W.V.'s official histories.

20. U.S.W.V., *Constitution*, pp. 13-15.

21. *Ibid.* 22. *Ibid.* 23 *Ibid.* 24. *Ibid.*, pp. 16-17.

25. As an example of its preoccupation with 1898, see *House Documents*, 85 Cong., 2 sess., No. 367, pp. 82-84. The 1957 National Encampment at Little Rock reiterated the constant theme: the righteousness of 1898, its glories, and its hardships.

26. U.S.W.V., *Constitution*, pp. 13-17. 27. *Ibid.*, p. 5.

28. *House Documents*, 68 Cong., 2 sess., No. 522, p. 203.

29. U.S.W.V., *Constitution*, p. 17.

30. *Ibid.*, p. 14; for an example of a jingoistic progressive see, Albert J. Beveridge, *The Meaning of the Times and other Speeches* (Indianapolis, 1908), pp. 47-57, 101-117; Hull House's Jane Addams and Stanford University's president David Starr Jordan were two progressives who were anti-imperialistic and anti-militaristic, see Jane Addams, *Newer Ideals of Peace* (London, 1907), pp. 3-61, and David Starr Jordan, *War and Waste; A Series of Discussions of War and War Accessories* (New York, 1913), pp. 52-64; also, Mowry, *The California Progressives*, pp. 87-104.

31. Harold Helfer related the story of the pledge of allegiance in "How the Pledge of Allegiance Came to Be Written," *The American Legion Magazine*, LIX (October, 1955), 14-15, 58-60. The pledge was written in 1892. Dearing, *Veterans in Politics*, pp. 472-474, describes the flag cult. Civil War veterans thought that a Flag Day would detract from Memorial Day; Davies, *Patriotism on Parade*, pp. 215-219. For the lack of military ritual, Millis, *Martial Spirit*, pp. 215-219; Walter Millis, *Arms and Men: A Study in American Military History* (New York, 1956), p. 301. McKinley's experience with the fleet was reported by *The New York Times*, September 8, 1899, 6:6.

32. Dearing, *Veterans in Politics*, pp. 86-87, 472-474.

33. Hermann Hagedorn, ed., *The Works of Theodore Roosevelt* (New York, 1925), XV, 15-31; XX, 457. Richard Hofstadter, *The American Political Tradition and the Men Who Made It* (New York, 1948), pp. 203-233 and Mowry, *The California Progressives*, pp. 87-104, suggest that Roosevelt epitomized American middle-class concern over the new society. In the literary field, such fears were expressed in Henry Brooks Adams, *The Education of Henry Adams; An Autobiography* (Boston and New York, 1918), and William Dean Howells, *A Hazard of New Fortunes* (New American ed., Clinton, Massachusetts, 1952).

34. W. M. Baker to the author, October 15, 1959, letter from the Recorder-in-Chief of the Naval and Military Order of the Spanish War. The Naval and Military Order was composed of officers and became an affiliate of the U.S.W.V.

35. *Ibid.*

36. V.F.W., Americanism, *The V.F.W. Story* pp. 1-2; Davies, *Patriotism on Parade*, p. 43.

37. V.F.W., Americanism, *The V.F.W. Story*, p. 1.

38. *Ibid.*   39. *Ibid.*, p. 2.   40. *Ibid.*

41. *Ibid.*, pp. 2-3. The changes in the V.F.W.'s concept of patriotism will be analyzed in later chapters.

42. U.S.W.V., *Constitution*, pp. 5, 17-18. For a discussion of militia versus Regular Army controversy which has existed since colonial days, see Millis, *Arms and Men*. The regular establishment has always disliked the power that the states have exercised over reserve units. It did manage to get rid of the volunteer regiments following the Spanish-American War, but it is still plagued by the highly political National Guard system.

43. The years prior to the First World War were often referred to as years of "discouragement" by the veterans in their attempts to coalesce and present a unified front. For an example, read comments by U.S.W.V. members at the 1924 Michigan City, Indiana, National Encampment; *House Documents*, 68 Cong., 2 sess., No. 522, p. 280. The slippery question of the veterans' groups relationship to authoritarian measures will be discussed in later chapters.

CHAPTER III

1. Arthur S. Link, *Woodrow Wilson and the Progressive Era, 1910-1917* (New York, 1954), pp. 145-173; George Kennan, *American Diplomacy*, pp. 55-73; Thomas A. Bailey, *Wilson and the Peacemakers* (New York, 1947), pp. 2-10.

2. Edward H. Buehrig, *Woodrow Wilson and the Balance of Power* (Bloomington, Indiana, 1955), pp. 106-169; Link, *Wilson and the Progressive Era*, pp. 145-173.

3. Buehrig, *Wilson and the Balance of Power*, p. 168; Link, *Wilson and the Progressive Era*, pp. 182-183, 252-282; Arthur S. Link, *Wilson the Diplomatist; A Look at His Major Foreign Policies* (Baltimore, 1957), pp. 13-22, 31-90.

4. For the defense policies of the Spanish-American War groups, see V.F.W. Americanism Commission, *The V.F.W. Story*, pp. 1-2, and U.S.W.V., *Constitution*, pp. 13-18. Roosevelt's views on defense and the policies of Wilson are in Theodore Roosevelt, *Fear God and Take Your Own Part* (New York, 1916), pp. 38-109, 116-137.

5. *Ibid.*; a self-expression of Roosevelt's views on military life and glory is found in *The Works of Theodore Roosevelt* (New York, 1906), XX, 25-38, 249-282; *ibid.*, XXI, 108-152, 219-226; also, George E. Mowry, *Theodore Roosevelt and the Progressive Movement* (American Century Series, New York, 1960), pp. 15, 309-313, 315-322; Henry Pringle, *Theodore Roosevelt, a Biography* (New York, 1931), pp. 126-140, 364-365, 412-420; William H. Harbaugh, *Power and Responsibility; the Life and Times of Theodore Roosevelt* (New York, 1961), pp. 93-107, 473-480; Richard Hofstadter, *The American Political Tradition and the Men Who Made It* (New York, 1948), pp. 209-215. America's entry into World War I and our military policies of that era are found in Buehrig, *Wilson and the Balance of Power*, p. 168; Link, *Wilson and the Progressive Era*, pp. 174-196; Walter Millis, *Arms and Men; a Study in America's Military History* (New York, 1956), pp. 190-191; Arthur Ekirch, Jr., *The Civilian and the Military* (New York, 1956), pp. 140-155.

6. Walter Millis, *Road to War; America 1914-1917* (New York, 1935), pp. 146-149; Hermann Hagedorn, *Leonard Wood; a Biography* (New York, 1931), II, 155.

7. *Ibid.*, pp. 155-156; *The New York Times*, March 1, 1915, 1:3; Arthur Sullivant Hoffman, "That Earlier American Legion," *The American Legion Magazine*, XVII (July, 1934), 12-13, 42-45.

8. *Ibid.*

9. *Literary Digest* (New York), March 13, 1915, pp. 532-533. The man who founded and named the Legion was Arthur Sullivant Hoffman, editor of *Adventure Magazine,* who had set out to form a military reserve in October, 1914. He was helped by Hausmann who introduced him to Wood on February 17, 1915. On February 19, Wood introduced Hoffman to Roosevelt; see Hoffman, *loc. cit.,* pp. 12, 13,, 42-45.

10. *The New York Times,* March 1, 1915, 1:3.

11. *New York County Records,* Borough of Manhattan, "Certification of Incorporation of American Legion," filed and recorded March 5, 1915, No. 1204-1915C, (original file No. 106/79467), pp. 1-5; see also, the New York *Tribune,* March 5, 1915, 3:1.

12. *The New York Times,* March 1, 1915, 4:2 see also, Hoffman, *loc. cit.,* pp. 12, 13, 42-45. Hoffman said that Cook wrote him in July, 1914 before the war became general. Hoffman likewise made no mention of Cook's ultimate fate.

13. Elting E. Morison and John M. Blum, eds., *The Selected Letters of Theodore Roosevelt* (Cambridge, 1951-1954), VIII, 909.

14. Hagedorn, *Leonard Wood,* II, 155-156; *Literary Digest* (New York), March 13, 1915, pp. 532-533; *Outlook* (New York), March 17, 1915, pp. 548-549.

15. The New York *American,* March 5, 1915, 18:1, and the New York *World,* March 4, 1915, 8:1; The New York *Herald,* March 4, 1915, 12:1, and March 7, 1915, 6:1-2.

16. Hagedorn, *Leonard Wood,* II, 155; *Literary Digest* (New York), March 13, 1915, pp. 532-533.

17. Quoted by Hagedorn in *Leonard Wood,* II, 156.

18. *Ibid.* Hagedorn's observation was that Wilson might have been justified. Hagedorn quoted Wood as saying that Wilson's personal ambitions overrode his sense of duty.

19. Hagedorn's comments on Wood's action in regard to the order from Garrison in *ibid.,* pp. 156-157.

20. Roosevelt to Dickinson, March 12, 1915, Theodore Roosevelt Letters.

21. Roosevelt to Dickinson, March 12, 1915, Roosevelt Letters; Millis, *Road to War,* pp. 148-149. It was unlikely that Wood was "obtuse." His eyes were on the White House. In 1920 he was a G.O.P. possibility; Hagedorn, *Leonard Wood,* II, 353-372.

22. Hagedorn, *Leonard Wood,* II, 155; *The Outlook* (New York), March 17, 1915, pp. 604-605; New York *Herald,* March 3, 1915, 6:5, March 4, 1915, 12:1; New York *American,* March 5, 1915, 18:1.

23. Roosevelt to Langdon Warner, an archaeologist married to Lorraine d'Oremieux Roosevelt, July 2, 1915, Roosevelt Letters.

24. Link, *Wilson and the Progressive Era,* pp. 185-186, and Samuel R. Spencer, *Decision for War, 1917; The Laconia Sinking and the Zimmermann Telegram as Key Factors in the Public Reaction Against Germany* (Rindge New Hampshire, 1953), pp. 34-35.

25. The name "Legion" was not new. Between 1900 and 1907 the Massachusetts Legion of Spanish War Veterans existed as a separate organization. In 1907, it was amalgamated with the U.S.W.V. The Massachusetts group was always referred to as the "Legion." In 1916, another "American Legion" appeared; Gregory Mason, "Crusaders of Today," *Outlook,* June 28, 1916, pp. 502-510. This Legion consisted of Americans serving in the 237th Battalion of the Canadian Army. The outfit was recruited by a Unitarian minister, the Reverend Doctor C. Seymour Bullock. Mason wrote that the title of "Legion" was not inappropriate," for the Legionnaires were

"Crusaders." The men, according to the article, fought for ". . . an abstract idea of justice and the satisfaction of their own consciences." It contained "over three thousand men" who were "modern knights-errant." The Legion's insignia was an incongruous one composed of George Washington's family coat of arms superimposed on the Canadian Maple Leaf.

26. See *infra*, pp. 38-41.

27. Link, *Wilson the Diplomatist*, pp. 12-22; Bailey, *Wilson and the Peacemakers*, p. 10; Link, *Woodrow Wilson and the Progressive Era*, pp. 266, 277; Kennan, *American Diplomacy*, pp. 65-68; Preston W. Slosson, *The Great Crusade and After* (New York, 1930), pp. 31-37; Hans Kohn, *American Nationalism; an Interpretive Essay* (New York, 1957), p. 204. Kohn likens Wilson's Americanism to Walt Whitman's, in that it identified the Ego with the American people, and the people with the cause of world freedom. This was partially true, but in fairness to Wilson, it must be pointed out that he was under no illusions as to the nature of an aroused, militant democracy. It compounded his tragedy. For an interesting view into the mind of a combat veteran describing militant zeal on behalf of Uncle Sam, see Marquis James, *A History of the American Legion* (New York, 1923), pp. 11-13. James, in contrast to the spate of war novels appearing in the twenties, glowingly recalls the elation felt by doughboys when they reached "a fighting man's estate" after Catigny, Belleau Wood, and Soissons. The soldiers were saviors, but only six months after November, 1918, their matchless morale was gone.

28. Leonard P. Ayers, *The War with Germany, a Statistical Summary* (Washington, 1919), pp. 11, 21; Marcus Duffield, *King Legion* (New York, 1931), pp. 193-197. Duffield's book represented the best written and best documented of the works generally unsympathetic to the Legion. For expressions of disgust with the war and disillusionment with postwar America by the literati, see Malcom Cowley, *Exile's Return* (New York, 1951); e. e. cummings, *The Enormous Room* (New York, 1934); John Dos Passos, *One Man's Initiation—1917* (London, 1920), *Three Soldiers* (New York, 1921), *U.S.A.—A Trilogy* (New York, 1937); Ernest Hemingway, *A Farewell to Arms* (New York, 1932), *In Our Time* (New York, 1925), *The Sun Also Rises* (New York, 1926); Laurence Stallings and Maxwell Anderson, *What Price Glory?* (New York, 1926). An excellent account and critical analysis of postwar American writers is in Frederick J. Hoffman, *The Twenties; American Writing in the Postwar Decade* (New York, 1955), pp. 47-54, 66-78, 122, 167, 379, 385-389, 391.

29. Millis, *Arms and Men*, p. 301; Slosson, *The Great Crusade*, pp. 31-71; Hoffman, *The Twenties*, pp. 66-78, 385-389. A valuable asset in the study of veterans' societies is Warner and Lunt, *Social Life of a Modern Community* I, 120-121. The two sociologists found that the American Legion was built around the crisis of World War I. That was the period when the entire community acted in concert. To recapture that sense of purpose and its resulting security, the Legion's ritual was designed to restate the behavior that occurred during the war crisis.

30. Duffield, *King Legion*, p. 194. For information concerning demobilization of the armed services and the flooding of the labor markets that could not assimilate the veterans, see James Robert Mock and Evangeline Thurber, *Report on Demobilization* (Norman, Oklahoma, 1944), pp. 133-134.

31. A literate, rational and well-documented study of the impact of war-time emotionalism upon the American pubic is in Zechariah Chafee, Jr., *Free Speech in the United States* (Cambridge, 1941), pp. 243-282.

32. Ole Hanson, "Bolshevism: This Old World Menace Will Find No Abiding Place in Free America," *The American Legion Weekly*, July 11, 1919, p. 13. For

further expressions of Hanson's views on Marxism, see Ole Hanson, *Americanism Versus Bolshevism* (New York, 1920). This book is an example of how the issue of Communism was exploited in a political sense.

33. Frederick Logan Paxson, *American Democracy and the World War* (Boston, 1939), III, 90-99. An invaluable contemporary account is in Commission of Inquiry, Interchurch World Movement, *Report on the Steel Strike of 1919* (New York, 1920).

34. Hanson, *loc. cit.*, p. 27.

35. Chafee, *Free Speech*, pp. 119, 141-195, 218-224; Paxson, *American Democracy*, III, 90-91; Slosson, *The Great Crusade*, pp. 72-104. For contemporary accounts of the Attorney General's "Red Hunt," see *The New York Times*, January 3, 1920, 1:5-7, 2:1-4, January 4, 1920, 1: 5-7, 2:1-5, January 5, 1920, 1:6-7, 2:1-2, 5-6.

36. James, *History of the Legion*, pp. 13, 15; Duffield, *King Legion*, p. 5.

37. An account of the Legion's "spontaneous" birth is in George S. Wheat, *The Story of the American Legion* (New York, 1919). Wheat's story is an eyewitness, contemporary one and full of the "gee-whiz" school of writing. The style is rhetorical, inflammatory in spots, and extremely partisan on behalf of the Legion.

38. James, *Story of the Legion*, pp. 14-16.

39. *Ibid.*, pp. 15-25; Justin Gray, *The Inside Story of the Legion* (New York, 1948), pp. 40-50. Gray was an idealistic and controversial World War II veteran who joined the Legion in 1946 and was assigned to its Americanism Commission branch at National Headquarters in Indianapolis. Perhaps he was too idealistic; in any case he became disillusioned about Legion national policy. He was the person who attempted to find if there was any link between the first and second Legions. He discovered references to it but said he was forbidden to examine the information further. Later he quit the Legion in disgust. An account of Pershing's and Wood's relations is in Hagedorn, *Leonard Wood*, II, 267-274. Wood never made mention of having anything to do with the second Legion. The position of Champ Clark, Jr., high in the Legion hierarchy, showed that Roosevelt fell over backwards to make the organization appear bi-partisan.

40. James, *History of the Legion*, pp. 16-19; Gray, *Inside Story of the Legion*, p. 48; *The American Legion Magazine*, XXXIV (January, 1943), 23-24; Hoffman, *loc. cit.*, pp. 44-45.

41. James, *History of the Legion*, pp. 20-22. Roosevelt was just in time to rescue his brother, Captain Archibald Roosevelt. Archibald had approved of the American Soldiers' and Sailors' Protective Association. Then, according to a press interview, Archibald Roosevelt heard that the Association adopted new aims. He withdrew his support in favor of "a new society" which had just been found overseas. See *The New York Times*, March 1, 1919, 7:1.

42. James, *History of the Legion*, pp. 23-25; Robert B. Pitkin, "When Teddy Said 'No!'," *The American Legion Magazine*, LXVI (May, 1959), 29-30. Legion accounts never mentioned the role of the first Legion save in a very few instances. In 1946, a history appeared written with Legion endorsement; Richard S. Jones, *History of the American Legion* (New York, 1946). By this time Gray had threatened to investigate the tie-up, and Jones' book made a brief mention of the first Legion. Any connection, however, between the two was treated as coincidence. Gray, his idealism soured by headquarters' mentality, darkly suspected that the first Legion may have been a private army of the elder Roosevelt's; Gray *Inside Story of the Legion*, p. 48; see *supra*, pp. 29-36.

43. James, *History of the Legion*, pp. 41-61; also Pitkin, *loc. cit.*, p. 29; for incorporation, *House Reports*, 66 Cong., 1 sess., No. 191, p. 2.

44. *Congressional Record,* LVIII, 4061-4075, August 20, 1919.

45. *House Documents,* 71 Cong., 3 sess., No. 576, p. vi; *Statutes at Large,* XLI, Part 1, 284-285; James, *History of the Legion,* pp. 60-62. The constitution's first draft was by Elihu Root, a member of the first Legion. James said that Root's draft did not "get to first base" because it "lacked the veterans' point of view."

CHAPTER IV

1. James, *History of the Legion,* pp. 41-61.

2. Arthur Warner, "The Truth About the American Legion," *The Nation,* July 6, 1921, pp. 7-10. Warner thought that European veteran societies were "progressive," but that the Legion was dominated by officers and "the silk stocking elements"; Warner, *The Nation,* July 13, 1921, p. 36. Warner called the Legion an "adjunct to the Republican Party" in New York. Many liberals, especially Warner, saw a connection between Theodore Roosevelt, Jr.'s political ambitions and the Legion. Roosevelt had been appointed Assistant Secretary of the Navy in 1921.

3. Millis, *Arms and Men,* pp. 241-243.

4. *Ibid.;* Oliver Lyman Spaulding, *The United States Army in War and Peace* (New York, 1937), pp. 451-467.

5. Millis, *Arms and Men,* p. 242.

6. Warner and Lunt, *Social Life of a Modern Community,* I, 118-119.

7. Military Order of the World War, *Minutes of the National Convention Held in Detroit, 1920* (New York, 1920), p. 8. (Hereafter cited as M.O.W.W., *Minutes*).

8. Recorder-General, Captain Sherrard Ewing, Infantry, United States Reserve, "Forward," *National Bulletin of the Military Order of the World War I* (1921), 3. (Hereafter cited as M.O.W.W., *National Bulletin*).

9. M.O.W.W., *Minutes, Detroit, 1920,* pp. 4-9. For an account of the Order of the Cincinnati, see Davies, *Patriotism on Parade,* pp. 1-27.

10. M.O.W.W., *Minutes, Detroit, 1920,* p. 8.

11. Warner, *Social Life of a Modern Community,* I, 116; Mead, *Keep Your Powder Dry,* p. 35.

12. M.O.W.W., *Minutes, Detroit, 1920,* pp. 8-9.

13. *Ibid.,* pp 73-77, 83-84 There were the usual restrictions against discussions of "sectarian" and "political partisanship" issues

14. *Ibid.*

15. Vice Commander-in-Chief, Mayor Almuth C. Vandiver, "Officer Obligations," M.O.W.W., *National Bulletin,* I (1921), 3.

16. M.O.W.W., *Minutes, Detroit, 1920,* pp. 8-9.

17. Commander-in-Chief George A. Harris, "Role of the Order," M.O.W.W. *National Bulletin,* II August, 1922, 7.

18. *Ibid.,* September, 1922, 7.

19. M.O.W.W., *Minutes, Detroit, 1920,* pp. 8, 73-74.

20. M.O.W.W., *National Bulletin,* II, August, 1922, 1.

21. M.O.W.W., *loc cit.,* IV, October, 1924, 1.

22. *Ibid.,* September, 1924, 7.   23. *Ibid.,* p. 3.

24. *Ibid.,* February, 1924, 2. It was possible that the M.O.W.W., being pledged to preserve and lead America as it should be led, was not in favor of feminism. It might have been hard for the military leaders to have had to share the leadership role with the newly enfranchised females of America.

25. M.O.W.W., *loc. cit.*, III, February, 1923, 6-7; *ibid.*, April, 1923, 6.

26. *Ibid.*, February, 1923, 3.   27. *Ibid.*, IV, January, 1924, 2.

28. *Ibid.*, February, 1924, 1; and May, 1924, 4.

29. *Ibid.*, February, 1924, 10.   30. *Ibid.*   31. *Ibid.*, March, 1924, 1-2.

32. M.O.W.W., *Minutes, Philadelphia, 1926*, p. 4. Colonel Hamilton Fish, Jr., also very active in Legion affairs (*supra*, p. 41), complained of the lack of members. Fish told his fellow M.O.W.W. comrades that something was wrong with "this great order" since it represented "only two per cent" of all the eligible officers who served in the First World War. He said that the M.O.W.W. did not possess the "influence and power" it should. Perhaps this was due, Fish said, to a confusion of names with the Veterans of Foreign Wars. Fish suggested that the M.O.W.W. change its name to the Order of Lafayette, which had greater sentimental value. For an example of those few who yelled when attacked by the M.O.W.W., see Norman Hapgood, *Professional Patriots* (New York, 1927), pp. 152-153, 169, 171-173. The rise of the military under the New Deal is discussed in Millis, *Arms and Men*, pp. 265-303.

33. James, *History of the Legion*, pp. 161-172. The Legion's allegations proved to have validity; Gustaufus A. Weber and Laurence F. Schmeckbier, *The Veterans' Administration; Its History, Activities and Organization* (Washington, 1934), pp. 89-114, 214-227.

34. *Ibid.* See also *House Documents*, 71 Cong., 2 sess., No. 494, pp. 2-3.

35. *Ibid.; House Documents*, 72 Cong., 2 sess., No. 450, pp. 102-112. For newspaper accounts, see *Christian Science Monitor* (Boston), June 28, 1921, 2:3, and June 29, 1921, 9:3, 20:3-5.

36. San Francisco *Chronicle*, June 26, 1922, 1:6, 2:1, 3, 4, 6, 3:1-8, 5:7; *House Documents*, 72 Cong., 2 sess., No. 450, pp. 102-112. The co-operation between the three groups centered around two policies common to them all. One was the maintenance of a strong national defense and the other was the annual "forget-me-not poppy" sales. Money earned from the sale of the poppies aided disabled veterans.

37. *House Documents*, 72 Cong., 2 sess., No. 450, pp. 102-112.

38. *Ibid.*

39. *House Documents*, 71 Cong., 2 sess., No. 494, p. 155.

40. *Ibid.*, pp. 3-4, 4-5, 94, 107. A Legionnaire told the D.A.V. in 1930, "we both are working toward the same end; we are working toward the betterment of the ex-service man . . ." For views on overlapping or dual membership, see Sam Stavisky, "The Veterans Make Their Choice," *Harper's Magazine*, CXCIII (1946), 251-258.

41. Marie Paula Dickoré, *The Order of the Purple Heart; An Account of Sergeant William Brown Who Brought His Badge of Merit to Columbus, Ohio* (Cincinnati, 1943), p. 9. (Hereafter cited as Dickoré, *Order of the Purple Heart*).

42. *Ibid.*, p. 12.

43. *Ibid.*, pp. 32-33; *The New York Times*, February 23, 1932, 1:1, 13: 1-8, made no mention of the Purple Heart; The Los Angeles *Times* made no editorial comment, but noted the Order's rebirth.

44. National Headquarters of the Military Order of the Purple Heart, *Summary of Proceedings of the Seventh National Encampment, San Francisco, August, 1939* (Gary, Indiana, 1939), pp. 66-67, 71, 78. (Hereafter cited as M.O.P.H., *Proceedings*). So inconspicuous was the M.O.P.H., that only one out of San Francisco's four daily papers bothered to report that it had met. Even then, the announcement consisted of one line of the smallest type buried in the back pages. San Francisco *Chronicle*, August 11, 1939, 25:6. By contrast, announcements of the forthcoming annual state

convention of the American Legion, Department of California, were printed. The San Francisco *News*, August 12, 1939, 1:5, 19:1-2.

CHAPTER V

1. Robert B. Pitkin, "How They Wrote the Preamble," *The American Legion Magazine*, LXVI (June, 1959), 31-32; James, *History of the Legion*, pp. 60, 81. One of the authors was Hamilton Fish, Jr., from New York.

2. Ivy Lee, "100 Per Cent Americanism," *The American Legion Weekly*, July 18, 1919, p. 7.

3. Robert B. Pitkin, "What Is 100 Per Cent Americanism?" *The American Legion Magazine*, LVII (May, 1954), 24-26; Hermann Hagedorn, *The Works of Theodore Roosevelt* (New York, 1925), XXI, 333.

4. *Supra*, pp. 25-26.

5. Roosevelt to Menken, January 10, 1917, Theodore Roosevelt Letters.

6. *Ibid.*

7. Theodore Roosevelt, *Fear God and Take Your Own Part* (New York, 1916), pp. 18-19, 42, 55, 105, 138-164; Roosevelt also denounced professional pacifists, greedy materialists, and "the mollycoddles of both sexes" and suggested peacetime conscription to help Americanize the immigrant and youth of the country and inculcate principles of "intense" and "exclusive loyalty to the United States." Almost the same wording was used by the M.O.W.W. thirty-eight years later in defense of a continued peacetime draft; M.O.W.W., *National Bulletin*, XXXV (November, 1954), 5-6. The hyphen was an issue in the election of 1916. Wilson was no less concerned than his political enemy Roosevelt with the problem; Albert Shaw, ed., *President Wilson's State Papers and Addresses* (New York, 1918), pp. 110, 132, 150, 293, 310; Link *Woodrow Wilson and Progressive Era*, pp. 246-247; Ray Stannard Baker, *Woodrow Wilson, Life and Letters; Facing War* (New York, 1937), VI 289-290.

8. New York *Tribune*, March 29, 1918, 1:1, 8:1-8, 9:1-2; San Francisco *Examiner*, March 29, 1928, 1:1, 2:7; *The Christian Science Monitor* (Boston), March 29, 1918, 4:2-3; Boston *Evening Transcript*, March 29, 1918, 1:3, 5:1-5; The *Evening Post* (New York), March 29, 1918, 6:5, 10:1, the *Post* was pro-Democratic; The *Evening Sun* (New York), March 29, 1918, 12:1. In 1952, a study was conducted that touched on several aspects of hyphenism. Hyphenates posed a real problem. They were not disloyal in the sense many citizens believed in 1917. They did, however, possess feelings and attitudes that ran counter to national policy. Irish-Americans had a deep mistrust of Britain. German-Americans tended to feel that the homeland had been unfairly treated. Our entry into the war was regarded by them as a piece of trickery, for in 1916 Wilson seemed to have promised to avoid war. Wartime discrimination solidified German-American resentment. Their antagonism was so intense that it helped to account for some of America's isolationist sentiment after 1917; Samuel Lubell, *The Future of American Politics* (New York, 1952), pp. 132-157.

9. American Legion National Headquarters, *Summary of Proceedings of the First National Convention, Indianapolis, November 11, 1919* (Indianapolis, 1919), p. 39. (Hereafter cited as Legion, *Summary of Proceedings*). The Legion's policy on immigration will be dealt with in a later chapter, *infra*, pp. 85-89.

10. Every issue of the *Weekly* during the years, 1919-1921, contained an article or a cartoon directed against alien slackers and conscientious objectors. For an account of the deportation drive, see Chafee, *Free Speech*, pp. 196-238, 240. The drive had

its roots in the war effort. As early as 1917, the Government prosecuted aliens who refused to serve. Chafee pointed out that public opinion was behind the Justice Department's actions; *The New York Times*, November 11, 1919, 10:1, 16:1-2. The *Times* reported that the assembled delegates in Indianapolis were told by Chairman Henry Lindsley that the Legion could "affect the trend of thought of the American people as no organization has ever done."

11. Charles D. Kelley, "A Starting Point for Slacker Drives," *The American Legion Weekly*, October 24, 1919, pp. 8,33-34.

12. *Congressional Record*, LXI, 8254-8263, June 7, 1921.

13. Hapgood, *Professional Patriots*, pp. 90-94.

14. *The American Legion Weekly*, December 26, 1919, p. 12; for a list of Legion lawlessness, see *The Literary Digest* (New York), November 29, 1919, pp. 19-20 and Duffield, *King Legion*, pp. 166-169.

15. *The American Legion Weekly*, February 3, 1920, p. 18.

16. *Ibid.*

17. Hapgood, *Professional Patriots*, pp. 57-58; see also Arthur Warner, "The Truth about the American Legion," *The Nation*, July 6, 1921, pp. 7-10. This article, one of a series on the Legion, was liberal in tone and reflected suspicion of the organization.

18. Hapgood, *Professional Patriots*, p. 57.

19. *The American Legion Weekly*, January 2, 1920, p. 20. One Indiana Legionnaire wrote in and protested against fellow Legionnaires who resorted to "mob rule" in breaking up socialist meetings. For further discussion on dissent with the Legion over Legion policies and actions, see *infra*, pp. 90-101.

20. Every National Convention from 1920 until the present (1962) has condemned the A.C.L.U. The Legion claimed that the A.C.L.U. "started in business" as "an outfit to aid draft dodgers in World War I." See *The American Legion Magazine*, LIX (September, 1955), 6. Legion records do not indicate any dissent from this view from within the organization.

21. *The American Legion Weekly*, February 3, 1920, p. 18; *Who's Who in America*, 1942-1943, p. 2394.

22. *The American Legion Weekly*, July 20, 1920, p. 29; *ibid.*, September 24, 1921, pp. 30-34.

23. Legion, *Summary of Proceedings*, 1923, *Indianapolis*, p. 62.

24. For an expression of American dislike for militarism, see *supra*, pp. 30-36, 43-50, Arthur A. Ekirch, Jr., *The Civilian and the Military* (New York, 1956), pp. 195-216. Ekirch contended that militarism gained a foothold it never lost due to World War I. He thought that Wilson tried to scare America into the League with the threat of future militarism if it did not join. A revival of anti-militarism was the work of "old-line liberals and pacifists aided by the rising tide of popular dissillusionment with the war," said Ekirch. See also Ekirch, *The Decline of American Liberalism* (New York, 1955), pp. 244-246. The liberal success against militarism was only temporary, Ekirch believed.

25. *Supra*, pp. 43-60.

26. M.O.W.W., *National Bulletin*, II (September, 1922), 7.

27. *Ibid.* See *The American Legion Weekly* issues from July, 1919 until December, 1919. All the issues carried advertisements to join the Legion which began "Do you know what you've got coming to you?" Humorous cartoons revolved around the enlisted man's traditional suffering under tough non-coms and green Second Lieutenants.

28. M.O.W.W., *loc. cit.*, p. 7.

29. Lindsey Blayney, "American Ideals and Traditions," *North American Review,* CCXV (1922), 577-589.

30. F. B. Kaye, "Americanism as an Educational Menace," *The Nation* (July 5, 1922), 11-12.

31. *House. Documents,* 68 Cong., 2 sess., No. 517, pp. 46, 132, 140-142; *ibid.,* 69 Cong., 1 sess., No. 243, pp. 140, 149; *ibid.,* 69 Cong., 2 sess., No. 553, pp. 76-77; *ibid.,* 68 Cong., 2 sess., No. 662, p. 61; *ibid.,* 69 Cong., 1 sess., No. 386, p. 205; *ibid.,* 68 Cong., 2 sess., No. 522, pp. 130-131.

32. *House Documents,* 69 Cong., 2 sess., No. 550, p. 183.

33. *Ibid.,* 70 Cong., 1 sess., No. 65, p. 112.

34. M.O.W.W., *Minutes, Seventh Annual Convention,* Baltimore, 1927, pp. 3-6.

35. Derden to the author, October 15, 1959, Letter from the National Adjutant of the U.S.W.V.

36. U.S.W.V., *National Headquarters, General Orders No. 3,* July 6, 1959, p. 1.

37. *Ibid.* Beneath the box containing the definition on the General Orders was a command that "the above definition is to be repeated in unison at every meeting of a camp." See also copies of the *House Documents* containing the annual Summary of Proceedings of the National Encampments of the U.S.W.V. since 1927.

38. *The Forum* (New York), LXXV (1926), 801-806.

39. *House Documents,* 72 Cong., 1 sess., No. 49, pp. 66-68, 219.

40. M.O.W.W., *Memorandum to All Members,* May 21, 1931.

41. M.O.W.W., *Minutes, Twelfth Annual Convention,* Washington, D.C., 1932, pp. 9-13. In 1939, Mosely was investigated for un-American activities by the United States Congress Mosely had been selected by George Deatherage, leader of the Knights of the White Camelia, to be the leader of a political party composed of patriotic groups. Deatherage was a founder of hate organizations. *House Special Committee on Un-American Activities Investigating Un-American Propaganda Within the United States,* 76 Cong., 1 sess., V, May 31, 1939, pp. 3545-3703.

42. Gray, *Inside Story of the Legion,* pp. 208-234. Gray, a former member of the Legion's National Americanism Commission, said that Chaillaux made use of such hate propaganda specialists as the Reverend Gerald L. K. Smith and the Reverend Gerald B. Winrod. Also Charles Guy Bolté, *The New Veteran* (New York, 1945), p. 63. Bolté was one of the founders of the liberal veterans' group known as the American Veterans Committee (A.V.C.), founded in 1944 (infra, p. 163). Bolté joined the Legion out of respect to his Legionnaire father. He made an investigation of all veterans' organizations before helping to found the A.V.C. He substantiated Gray's charges and said that Chaillaux distributed hate group literature to the various posts within the Legion.

43. National Americanism Commission of the American Legion, *Isms; A Review of Revolutionary Communism and Its Active Sympathizers in the United States* (Indianapolis, 1936), 287 pp. (Hereafter cited as *Isms*). Chaillaux's activities as a Director will be discussed in a later chapter. *Infra,* pp. 54-71, 90-101.

44. Cyrus LeRoy Baldridge, "Americanism—What Is It?" reprinted in *The New Republic,* July 8, 1936, pp. 268-269; also Baldridge, "Is the American Legion American?" *Scribner's Magazine,* C (1936), 134-138; *The New Republic* (New York), June 3, 1936, p. 87. For newspaper comment, *The New York Times,* May 22, 1936, 25:6, and May 23, 1936, 17:5.

45. Baldridge, "Is the American Legion American?" *loc. cit.,* pp. 134-138. *The New York Times,* May 22, 1936, 25:6.

46. *The New Republic*, June 3, 1936, p. 87.

47. Baldridge, *loc. cit.*, p. 138.

48. *House Documents*, 75 Cong., 1 sess., No. 41, pp. 16, 131. By 1955, Murphy found himself in Baldridge's position. He headed a committee to investigate the UNESCO program. The Legion's hierarchy tabled his report which favored UNESCO; *infra*, pp. 98-99.

49. An excellent analysis of how a pressure group operates is found in David Bicknell Truman, *The Governmental Process: Political Interests and Public Opinion* (New York, 1951), pp. 141-142. Truman examined the "King-Makers" of the Legion. A dated, but still valuable, review of the sociological background of the Legion's hierarchy during the twenties and thirties is in William Gellerman, *The American Legion as Educator* (New York, 1938), pp. 54-65. Gellerman examined the social and economic background of the Legion's first twenty-one National Commanders. They were generally Protestant, well situated financially, and college graduates for the most part. By contrast, the average Legionnaire was a wage worker. The Legion "King-Makers" had the time and money to be leaders. To make sure that it will have a steady crop of professional Legionnaires, the Legion started its own American Legion College for specially selected personnel. The college is at National Headquarters in Indianapolis; National Headquarters of the American Legion, *The National Legionnaire*, May 6, 1946, 2:5. (Hereafter cited as *National Legionnaire*).

50. For a sociological view of veteran society membership, see *supra*, pp. 19-20, Robert S. Lynd and Helen Merrell Lynd, *Middletown in Transition; A Study in Cultural Conflicts* (New York, 1937), pp. 85, 92, 110-111, 217, 321, 407, 415, 429, 507, 510. The Lynds' study corroborated Warner's "Yankee City" series in regard to patriotic society membership. The Legion had a high degree of acceptance by the community and its concept of Americanism was respected. The Lynds found that the major attraction of the local veterans' post was its social program and spirit of "in-group" feeling.

51. For examples of dissatisfaction on the part of Legionnaires and V.F.W. comrades with headquarters' policies, see *infra*, pp. 143-146; Truman, *Governmental Process*, pp. 141-142, 151, 186-187, 197, 207, 242, 317, 336; Duffield, *King Legion*, pp. 110-111, 299.

52. Eric F. Goldman, *Rendezvous with Destiny; A History of Modern American Reform* (New York, 1953), pp. 374-390.

53. *House Documents*, 76 Cong., 3 sess., No. 750, pp. 128-134, 145-149; *ibid.*, 77 Cong., 1 sess., No. 38, pp. 285, 306; M.O.P.H., *Proceedings, Seventh Annual National Encampment*, San Francisco, 1939, pp. 66. 66-78, 111. (Hereafter cited as M.O.P.H., *Proceedings*); The San Francisco *Chronicle*, August 11, 1939, 25:6. The *Chronicle* used one stick of its smallest type to list the event. By contrast, the Legion's California Department was in the process of assembling for its annual convention and before the local Legion held its first session it monopolized the news. San Francisco *News*, August 12, 1939, 1:5, 19:1. The best analysis of the Legion's official shift from isolation is found in Roscoe Baker, *The American Legion and American Foreign Policy* (New York, 195), pp. 155-186.

54. *House Documents*, 76 Cong., 3 sess., No. 953, pp. 68-71.

55. *Ibid.*   56. *Ibid.*

57. *House Documents*, 76 Cong., 3 sess., No. 985, pp. 171-175.

58. *Ibid.*

59. Henry C. Fuller, Sr., National Americanism Director, "Americanization," *The Purple Heart*, V (January, 1944), 8-10.

60. *House Documents*, 79 Cong., 1 sess., No. 368, pp. 60-61.

61. *House Documents*, 82 Cong., 2 sess., No. 319, p. 178.

62. *House Documents*, 84 Cong., 1 sess., No. 55, pp. 165-172.

63. Pitkin, *loc. cit.*, pp. 24-26.

64. *The American Legion Magazine*, LXIV (January, 1958), 1.

65. Comparisons of the various Americanism programs will be found *infra*, pp. 72-89.

66. *Infra*, p. 72.

67. M.O.W.W., *National Bulletin*, XXXV (November, 1954), 2-6. What bothered Maas the most was the Budget Bureau's curtailment of medical and P.X. services, plus the drop-off in appointments to the service academies.

CHAPTER VI

1. Dearing, *Veterans in Politics*, pp. 472-488; *House Documents*, 68 Cong., 2 sess., No. 522, pp. 130-131; *ibid.*, 71 Cong., 3 sess., No. 575, pp. 114-115; *ibid.*, 72 Cong. 1 sess., No. 47, p. 140; *ibid.*, 74 Cong., 2 sess., No. 47, p. 140; *ibid.*, 74 Cong., 2 sess., No. 348, pp. 123-125, for the year 1935 In 1957, the U.S.W.V. was told by its Patriotic Instructor, John H. Rawlins, that he received "only two full reports"; "age and infirmities" caused this, it was reported, but "the spirit of patriotism was as strong as ever"; *ibid.*, 85 Cong., 2 sess., No. 367, p. 187.

2. *Ibid.*, 68 Cong., 2 sess., No. 662, p. 61; *ibid.*, 69 Cong., 1 sess., No. 789, pp. 52, 206-208, 222-223; *ibid.*, 70 Cong., 1 sess., No. 268, pp. 113, 211, 272, 274.

3. National Department of Americanism of the V.F.W., *Etiquette of the Stars and Stripes* (Kansas City, Missouri, 1959), pp. 2, 20; The National Americanism Commission of the American Legion, *Americanism Manual* (Indianapolis, Indiana, 1953), pp. 32-40; *House Documents*, 69 Cong., 1 sess., No. 789, pp. 52, 206-208.

4. M.O.W.W., *National Bulletin*, II (August, 1922), 7. For the M.O.W.W.'s counter-subversion activities, *infra*, pp. 140-141. M.O.W.W., *Minutes of General Staff Meeting*, October 6, 1926, 1926, p. 2.

5. *House Documents*, 74 Cong., 1 sess., No. 46, pp. 140-142; for further information of the McCormack-Dickstein investigation, *infra*, p. 93. *House Documents*, 76 Cong., 3 sess., No. 985, pp. 171-175; in 1940, the D.A.V. urged its members to support the M.O.W.W.'s special campaign to legalize Army Day, April 6, as an official patriotic observance; *D.A.V. Semi-Monthly* March 14, 1940, 2:1.

6. American Legion, *Summary of Proceedings*, Minneapolis, November, 1919, p. 39.

7. *Supra*, pp. 57-59. Duffield, *King Legion*, pp. 166-169; *The Literary Digest* (New York), November 29, 1919, pp. 19-20.

8. *The American Legion Weekly*, September 26, 1919, p. 12.

9. James, *History of the Legion*, p. 300; *The American Legion Weekly*, February 13, 1920, p. 18; *ibid.*, April 23, 1920, p. 7.

10. *The American Legion Weekly*, June 3, 1921, p. 20.

11. *Ibid.*

12. *Ibid.*, April 1, 1921, p. 9. The Legion's budget figures were contained in

National Treasurer's Reports to the National Convention of the American Legion, *House Documents,* 68th to 85th Congresses. Washington, 1924-1957. The Legion's percentage of funds spent on Americanism remained fairly constant over a thirty year period. Inflation, however, and rising costs caused the amounts of money spent to increase. In 1924, the Americanism Commission spent $13,000 on Americanism. In 1957, it spent close to $120,000. Figures spent on Americanism by the other societies were more difficult to ascertain. The U.S.W.V., D.A.V., M.O.P.H, M.O.W.W., and A.V.C. did not report funds spent on Americanism projects. Such items were carried as headquarters' expenses. As they possessed no formal programs, the amounts probably were small. The American Veterans of World War II and Korea spent approximately $25,000 from 1955 to 1957 in the creation of an Americanism program, see *infra,* pp. 108-111. The V.F.W.'s Americanism budgets paralleled the Legion's. From 1934 to 1937, it averaged over three per cent of its annual budgets on Americanism activities; *House Documents,* 75 Cong., 3 sess., No. 466, pp. 101-102. In 1957, the percentage allotted was three per cent. Like the Legion, the V.F.W. contended with inflation. In 1937, it spent over $10,000. Twenty years later its programs cost close to $49,000; *House Documents,* 85 Cong., 2 sess., No. 305, p. 267.

13. *House Documents,* 74 Cong., 1 sess., No. 45, pp. 177-178, 213-219.

14. *Ibid.,* 84 Cong., 1 sess., No. 55, pp. 165-171. The Legion's program was contained in National Americanism Commission of the American Legion, *Americanism Manual* (Indianapolis, 1953), p. 12. (Hereafter cited as *Manual*).

15. *Ibid.*   16. *Ibid.*

17. American Legion, *Constitution and By-Laws* (Indianapolis, 1958), pp. 3-9; National Americanism Commission, *Manual,* p. 7.

18. American Legion, *Constitution,* pp. 9-12; *House Documents,* 85 Cong., 2 sess., No. 303, pp. 461-463.

19. American Legion, *Constitution,* p. 10; Gray, *Inside the Legion,* pp. 165-172, 209-212, 217-219, 229.

20. National Americanism Commission, *Manual,* p. 7.

21. *Ibid.,* pp. 7-8. The Legion attempted to keep continuity by a system of executive committees. All past commanders of any type of unit or level automatically become members of the Legion's various executive committees; interview with Legionnaire William Swinehart, May 3, 1960, San Mateo, California. Swinehart, an enthusiastic Legionnaire, was a World War II veteran who took his Legion membership seriously. As a member of San Mateo Post No. 82, he was a frequent delegate to the county, departmental, and national conventions. See also, Bolte, *The New Veteran,* p. 59.

22. *House Documents,* 85 Cong., 2 sess., No. 303, pp. 53-60; the 1957 national convention illustrated how resolutions were presented. The convention's Americanism Committee chairman simply read the resolutions off and asked for acceptance. *Supra,* pp. 64-66, and *infra,* pp. 91-95.

23. Interview with Legionnaire William Swinehart, May 3, 1960, San Mateo, California. Swinehart's explanation of the suffrage system was detailed. He said that the post commander and the seven executive officers "automatically" attended all conventions. Other delegates were selected, but usually by the executive officers. Posts with over a thousand members usually could afford to provide their delegates with a convention budget. Swinehart said that as far as he knew this practice was restricted to Illinois and Pennsylvania. The average post was too poor to provide any funds for the delegates so they paid their own way. Swinehart's comments indicated

that delegates were usually men with the money and leisure time to attend conventions. Possibly, this might indicate the conservatism of the convention resolutions. Bolté, *The New Veteran*, pp. 59-61.

24. Unanimity of opinion might also be explained partially by the sociological makeup of the delegates. Judged by William Swinehart's remarks, the delegates were inclined to be those types of Legionnaires who possessed an approving, professional interest in the organization. National Legion leaders appeared to be drawn from such a *milieu;* see also William Gellermann, *The American Legion as Educator* (New York, 1938), pp. 52-67. Gellermann's book, though dated, retains value. He conducted a sociological analysis of the Legion's first twenty-two national commanders. All were "well situated economically," generally Protestant in religious affiliation, college graduates, oriented toward the business world, and interested in civic affairs. Also, Bolté, *The New Veteran*, p. 59. National Americanism Commission, *Manual*, pp. 5-6; Gray, *Inside the Legion*, pp. 31, 35-36, 209-213. Gray's esteem for his fellow Americanism experts was not high. He considered most to be reactionary and rather ignorant. Chuck Wilson, Gray's superior, was a professional Legionnaire. He started as an mail clerk at national headquarters in 1923. During World War II he was the Americanism Commission's assistant director. Gray claimed that Wilson was obsessed with the idea that the Y.M.C.A. was a Communist front organization.

25. The biggest differences between the two largest societies and the others lie in terminology and size. The D.A.V., M.O.W.W., and M.O.P.H have dispensed with departments. They are organized into geographic districts that might include several states. Within these areas the members form chapters. The U.S.W.V. is organized on a departmental basis but refers to its lowest units as camps. The A.V.C. is divided into area councils within metropolitan centers. Chapters are formed within the councils. None of the societies possess the mass of executive committees so prevalent in the Legion. The D.A.V.'s case is representative In 1957, it maintained five national executive committees, and had eight national officers; *House Documents*, 85 Cong., 2 sess., No. 307, p. viii. The Legion, by contrast, had eight national officers, twelve national commissions, and thirty-eight national standing committees; *ibid.*, 85 Cong., 2 sess., No. 303, pp. 481-482.

26. *Ibid.*, 85 Cong., 2 sess., No. 305, pp. 150, 199-203.

27. James, *History of the Legion*, pp. 161-165, 306; American Legion, *Summary of Proceedings*, Cleveland, 1920, p. 58.

28. *House Documents*, 68 Cong., 2 sess., No. 517, pp. 7-9, 64, 70-79, 83, 88, 132, 140.

29. *Ibid.*, 69 Cong., 1 sess., No. 243, pp. 140-149. An educator, William Gellermann, was critical of the Legion's sales technique in regard to its Americanism program. See William Gellermann, *The American Legion as Educator* (New York, 1938), pp. 81-82.

30. *House Documents*, 69 Cong., 2 sess., No. 553, pp. 76-77, 81, 83.

31. *Ibid.*, 69 Cong., 1 sess., No. 52, pp. 52, 206-208; *ibid.*, 84 Cong., 1 sess., No. 55, pp. 165-167; Americanism Commission, *Manual*, pp. 13-15; V.F.W., Department of Americanism, *The V.F.W. A Good Outfit* (Kansas City, Missouri, 1959), pp. 1-7.

32. Appreciation for the community service work was found in Willard W. Waller, *The Veteran Comes Back* (New York, 1944), pp. 208-209. For an opposing view, see Gellermann, *The Legion as Educator*, pp. 3-75, 238-266.

33. *House Documents*, 76 Cong., 1 sess., No. 39, pp. 163-174, and *The National Legionnaire*, VI (March, 1940), 4, 12.

34. *House Documents*, 84 Cong., 1 sess., No. 55, pp. 165-167, and *ibid.*, 76 Cong.,

1 sess., No. 39, pp. 163-174; Americanism Commission, *Manual*, p. 13; *The National Legionnaire*, VI (March, 1940), 4, 12.

35. Americanism Commission, *Manual*, p. 15.

36. *House Documents*, 81 Cong., 2 sess., No. 734, pp. 25-38, 131-140. *The American Legion Magazine*, LXIII (January, 1955), 33-34.

37. *Publisher's Weekly* (New York), September 13, 1952, pp. 1005-1006. Carl Knudson, "Are Legion Chaplains Yes Men?" *Christian Century*, December 11, 1950, pp. 15, 39-40.

38. *House Documents*, 69 Cong., 1 sess., No. 243, p. 140; Americanism Commission, *Manual*, p. 44. *Gray Inside the Legion*, p. 204.

39. *House Documents*, 68 Cong., 2 sess., No. 662, p. 61; *ibid.*, 69 Cong., 1 sess., No. 268, pp. 113, 211, 272, 274; *ibid.*, 68 Cong., 2 sess., No. 517, p. 122.

40. *Ibid.*, 68 Cong., 2 sess., No. 522, p. 190; *ibid.*, 76 Cong., 3 sess., No. 985, pp. 171-175.

41. *Ibid.*, 77 Cong., 2 sess., No. 537, p. 111. Robert B. Pitkin, "The American Legion and the Schools," *The American Magazine*, LXIX (September, 1959), 24-25, 26, 40-41.

42. Pitkin, *loc. cit.*, pp. 40-41. Charles G. Bolté, *The New Veteran* (New York, 1945), p. 56; Gray, *Inside the Legion*, pp. 212, 236-237. John Dixon, "What's Wrong with U. S. History?" *The American Legion Magazine*, XLVI (May, 1949), pp. 16, 40-41; Americanism Commission, *Manual*, p. 13.

43. Joseph Keeley, "Let's Have More Schools Like This!" *The American Legion Magazine*, LI (August, 1951), 16, 26-30.

44. M.O.W.W., *Minutes*, Executive Meeting, November 9, 1948, p. 6; M.O.W.W., *National Bulletin*, XXXIV (February, 1955), 2. Pitkin, *loc. cit.*, pp. 24-25, 26, 40-41.

45. Gellermann, *The Legion as Educator*, pp. v, 221-227.

46. Americanism Commission, *Manual*, p. 13; Department of Americanism, *The V.F.W. A Good Outfit*, pp. 3-7; M.O.W.W., *National Bulletin*, II (August, 1922), p. 7; U.S.W.V., *Constitution*, p. 14; *House Documents*, 76 Cong., No. 985, pp. 171-175. C. E. Scoogins, "Who Was George Rogers Clark?" *The American Legion Monthly*, IV (February, 1928), 18-19, 52-62; Kenneth Foree, "The Flag That Wouldn't Come Down!" *The American Legion Magazine*, XLVIII (June, 1950), 11-13, 48-49; Mancel Talcott, "Known But to God," *The American Legion Magazine*, XLIX (November, 1950), 24, 45-46; Clarence Manion, "We Can Win with These Terms!" *The American Legion Magazine*, LI (July, 1951), 9, 48; Harold G. Stagg, "Is the Medal of Honor Being Cheapened?" *The American Legion Magazine*, LI (October, 1951), 26, 27, 28; M. A. Hancock, "Hello Johnny Reb," *The American Legion Magazine*, LXIII (November, 1957), 24-25, 46-48. Also, Gellermann, *The Legion as Educator*, pp. 217-221.

47. Americanism Commission, *Manual*, pp. 6, 40-42. In 1931. Comrade Christopher G. Beres, a naturalized citizen and member of the V.F.W., told the delegates to the thirty-second National Encampment that immigrants "who are not willing to share our responsibility" should be "taken by the ears" and "kicked" back to "where they came from." See *House Documents*, 72 Cong., 1 sess., No. 49, p. 18. Today the Legion feels that the problem of Americanizing the immigrants in public schools has "almost wholly vanished." Pitkin, *loc. cit.* pp. 24-26, 40-41.

48. *The American Legion Weekly*, January 30, 1920, p. 10. Oscar Handlin, *The Uprooted; The Epic Story of the Great Migrations That Made the American People*

(New York, 1951), pp. 272-285; Eric F. Goldman, *Rendezvous with Destiny* (New York, 1953), pp. 299-300.

49. *The American Legion Weekly*, April 29, 1921, pp. 5-6. Also, *House Documents*, 68 Cong., 2 sess., No. 517, pp. 136-137.

50. *The American Legion Weekly*, July 2, 1920, p. 16; *ibid.*, August 13, 1920, p. 13.

51. *House Documents*, 68 Cong., 2 sess., No. 517, pp. 136-143.

52. *Congressional Record*, LXV, January 7, 1924, 580. For a detailed study of the Legion's pressures on Congress, the executive branch of the Federal Government and the American public in regard to foreign policy and immigration affairs, see Roscoe Baker, *The American Legion and Foreign Policy* (New York, 1954), pp. 51-82. *The American Legion Weekly*, January 13, 1922, p. 6; *ibid.*, November 5, 1920, pp. 3-4.

53. *House Documents*, 68 Cong., 2 sess., No. 517, pp. 136-143; William S. Bernard, ed., *American Immigration Policy—A Reappraisal* (New York, 1950), pp. 19, 23-31, 111-121; John Higham, *Strangers in the Land; Patterns of American Nativism* (New Brunswick, New Jersey, 1955), pp. 224, 256, 313, 322-326.

54. Americanism Commission, *Manual*, pp. 41-42. The Legion has remained silent on two aspects of the McCarran-Walter Act. The act's quota system came from the 1924 National Origins bill. Students of immigration policies claimed that the quotas discriminated against European Catholics. The McCarran Act, however, did remove total Asian exclusion. Japanese, as an example, were admitted under quotas; Stewart G. Cole and Mildred Wiese Cole, *Minorities and the American Promise; The Conflict of Principle and Practice* (New York, 1954), pp. 136-137, 148-153, 242.

55. Americanism Commission, *Manual*, p. 41. *House Documents*, 80 Cong., 1 sess., No. 470, pp. 227-230. Also *ibid.*, 84 Cong., 1 sess., No. 54, pp. 97-101.

56. *Ibid.*, 71 Cong., 2 sess, No 494, p. 49; *ibid.*, 72 Cong., 1 sess., No. 49, p. 66; Courtland to the Order, August 31, 1931, Memorandum from the Adjutant General's Office of the M.O.W.W.

57. *The New Republic*, May 26, 1952, p. 5; also *Commonweal* (New York), June 3, 1952, pp. 263-265. Morton Grodzins, *Americans Betrayed; Politics and the Japanese Evacuation* (Chicago, 1949), pp. 1-91. *House Documents*, 77 Cong., 1 sess., No. 296, p. 80; United States Congress, *House Committee on Immigration and Naturalization, Repeal of the Chinese Exclusion Acts*, 1943, p. 168; California Department, American Legion, *Summary of Proceedings*, San Francisco, August, 1943, pp. 66-67; *House Documents*, 78 Cong., 1 sess., No. 364, p. 339; *Congressional Record*, LXXXIX, 9992, November 26, 1943.

58. *The American Legion Weekly*, April 8, 1921, p. 10. Handlin, *The Uprooted*, pp. 272-285, 300; also Warner and Lunt, *Social Life of a Model Community*, I, 118-119; Fillmore H. Sanford, *Authoritarianism and Leadership; A Study of the Follower's Orientation to Authority* (Philadelphia, 1950), pp. 26-27, 43-44, 76-77, 94-95, 146-147; C. Wright Mills, *White Collar; The American Middle Classes* (New York, 1956), pp. 3-12, 239-286; Goldman, *Rendezvous with Destiny*, pp. 298-306.

59. *The American Legion Weekly*, April 8, 1921, p. 10.

60. Goldman, *Rendezvous with Destiny*, pp. 298-306. Handlin, *The Uprooted*, pp. 269, 272-273, 281-285.

61. Americanism Commission, *Manual*, p. 42.

62. Hapgood, *Professional Patriots*, pp. 61-63; Duffield, *King Legion*, pp. 193-222, 298-315; Gellermann, *The Legion as Educator*, pp. 238-266. *The National Legionnaire*, II (April, 1936), 3. Descriptions of V.F.W. naturalization ceremonies were contained

in *House Documents,* 75 Cong., 1 sess., No. 39, p. 206; Americanism Commission, *Manual,* p. 42.

CHAPTER VII

1. Hapgood, *Professional Patriots,* pp. 56-63, 171-173; Duffield, *King Legion,* pp. 156-191. National Americanism Commission of the American Legion, *Isms: A Review of Revolutionary Communism and Its Active Sympathizers in the United States* (Indianapolis, 1936), pp. 287. Gray, *Inside the Legion,* pp. 180-190. Carlson, *The Plotters,* pp. 252-255. For the N.C.U.L.L.'s fate, see *infra,* p. 105.

2. M.O.W.W., *National Bulletin,* III (March, 1923), 2, 6. *House Documents,* 70 Cong., 2 sess., No. 288, pp. 108-114. *Ibid,* 76 Cong, 3 sess., No 953, pp. 68-71; *ibid.,* 77 Cong., 1 sess., No. 406, pp. 173-183. Also, Baker, *American Legion and Foreign Policy,* pp. 26-27.

3. *Supra,* pp. 9-12, 20, 37-38, 55-58. American Legion Americanism Commission, *Manual,* pp. 1-7, 22, 33-34. V.F.W. Americanism Department, *The V.F.W., A Good Outfit,* pp. 1-7. *House Documents,* 69 Cong., 2 sess., No. 550, pp. 180-183; *ibid.,* 70 Cong., 1 sess., No. 65. *The New Republic,* May 18, 1932, p. 22; Gellermann, *The Legion as Educator,* pp. 87-134.

4. M.O.W.W., *Bulletin,* IV (February, 1924), 1-2. *House Documents,* 68 Cong., 2 sess., No. 517, p. 129; *ibid.,* 68 Cong., 2 sess., No. 522, p. 83. MOWW, *Bulletin,* III (February, 1923), 7.

5. M.O.W.W., *Bulletin,* IV (February, 1924), 1-2; *ibid.,* XXXIV (January, 1959), 6; *ibid.,* XXXIV (May, 1959), 7.

6. *House Documents,* 69 Cong., 1 sess., No. 243, p. 149; also Hapgood, *Professional Patriots,* pp. 59-60. Roy H. Abrams, What Happened at West Chester," *The Christian Century,* XLIV (1927), 849-850. Duffield, *King Legion,* pp. 228-229, 293-297. Report of the Special Investigating Committee, *Imperial Valley Farm Situation* (Sacramento, California, 1934), pp. 8-12; Gray, *Inside the Legion,* pp. 138-139. San Francisco *Chronicle,* July 4, 1934, p. 5; San Francisco *Examiner,* July 4, 1934, p. 6; Paul Eliel, *The Waterfront and General Strikes* (San Francisco, 1934).

7. Gray, *Inside the Legion,* pp. 208-209. Gray's charge was sustained by Edward Levinson, *Labor on the March* (New York, 1938), pp. 187-235. Carlson, *The Plotters,* pp. 198-200.

8. Gellermann, *The Legion as Educator,* pp. 264-266. Also, United States Congress, *House Special Committee on Un-American Activities Investigating Propaganda Within the United States,* 73 Cong., 2 sess., Public Hearings No. 73, pp. 17-20.

9. *The New York Times,* May 16, 1941, 25:3; John Roy Carlson, pseud., (Arthur Derounian), *Undercover; My Four Years in the Nazi Underworld of America* (Philadelphia and New York, 1943), pp. 188-192. Carlson's book was started with the help of *Fortune Magazine's* editor, Russell Davenport. *House Documents,* 78 Cong., 1 sess., No. 364, pp. 95-96; *Newsweek Magazine* (Dayton, Ohio), March 2, 1942, p. 29; *ibid.,* March 23, 1942, pp. 24-25; Gray, *Inside the Legion,* pp. 218-219. The American Legion, California Department Americanism Committee, 17 District, Los Angeles, *Report No. 3; The Case of Hamilton Fish* (Los Angeles, 1944), pp. 3-16.

10. M.O.W.W., *Minutes,* National Convention, Washington, D.C., 1932, pp. 66-70. One of the men who argued against Belknap wished to abolish Congress. He said that pacifists might gain too much power over the lawmakers.

11. *House Documents,* 77 Cong., 1 sess., No. 406, pp. 173-183. The Disabled Ameri-

can Veterans' *Monthly* (Cincinnati), XXXVIII (October, 1959), 1, 2; Carlson, *The Plotters*, pp. 309-310.

12. Morton Grodzins, *Americans Betrayed; Politics and the Japanese Evacuation* (Chicago, 1949), pp. 38-43, 44-45, 55, 174-179, 218-219; Gwynne Nettler, "The Relationship Between Attitude and Information Concerning the Japanese in America" (Ph.D. dissertation, Stanford University, 1945), pp. 10-20, 29-60. *House Documents*, 77 Cong., 2 sess., No. 896, pp. 77, 80. Eugene V. Rostow, "Our Worst Wartime Mistake," *Harper's Magazine*, CXCI (1945), 193-201; *The New Republic*, November 6, 1944, p 598; *The New York Times*, December 15, 1944, 13:5.

13. *The New York Times*, January 27, 1954, 1:1; *ibid.*, January 29, 1954, 18: 2-3. George Groh, "Norwalk, N.A.T.O., and the V.F.W.: 'What's All the Hollering?'" *The Reporter Magazine*, March 16, 1954, pp. 28-31; *The New Republic*, February 8, 1954, p. 4; *Commonweal* (New York), February 12, 1954, p. 465; Bernard DeVoto, "Norwalk and Points West," *Harper's Magazine*, CCVIII (1954), 10-15. *House Documents*, 84 Cong., 1 sess., No. 55, pp. 168, 172.

14. Gellermann, *The Legion as Educator*, pp. 46-49, 264-266; Gray, *Inside the Legion*, pp. 207-238. Alvin Owsley's comment was quoted in Duffield, *King Legion*, pp. 168-169.

15. Gray, *Inside the Legion*, pp. 222-234; Gellermann, *The Legion as Educator*, pp. 240, 241-253, 264-266; Duffield, *King Legion*, pp. 172-192; *The New Republic*, November 6, 1944, p. 598. The 1940 G.O.P. Presidential nominee, Wendell L. Willkie, blamed the 1943 Detroit race riots on "a fascist state of mind"; *The New York Times*, July 25, 1943, 25:2; Alfred McClung Lee and Norman Daymond Humphrey, *Race Riot* (New York, 1943), pp. 4, 5-6, 13-18, 63-64, 97, 111-113; Jack Goodman, ed., *While You Were Gone; A Report on Wartime Life in the United States* (New York, 1946) pp. 89-111; *The Nation*, June 5, 1943, pp. 794-795; *The New Republic*, June 21, 1943, pp. 818-820; *ibid.*, June 28, 1943, p. 845; *The Christian Century Magazine*, June 16, 1943, pp. 724-725, 726; *ibid.*, June 23, 1943, pp. 733-734, 735-736, 759-761; *Commonweal*, June 25, 1943, pp. 243-244; *ibid.*, July 2, 1943, p. 263.

16. T. W. Adorno, *et al.*, *The Authoritarian Personality* (New York, 1950), 2 vols. Also, Fillmore H. Sanford, *Authoritarianism and Leadership; A Study of the Follower's Orientation to Authority* (Philadelphia, 1950), pp. 7-174; and Harold W. Metz and Charles A. Thomson, *Authoritarianism and the Individual* (Washington, D.C., 1950).

17. Adorno, *et al.*, *Authoritarian Personality*, I, ix.

18. *Ibid.*, 222-279.

19. Sanford, *Authoritarianism and Leadership*, pp. 14, 26-27, 43-44, 76-77, 94-95, 120, 125-126, 146-147, 171-174.

20. *Supra*, pp. 38-40, 45-50. Eugene Lyons, "Why the Reds Are Gaining in America," *The American Legion Magazine*, LXVII (October, 1959), 18-19. Also M.O.W.W., *National Bulletin*, XXXIV (January, 1959), 6; *ibid.*, XXXIV (February, 1959), 1-2; *ibid.*, XXXIV (May, 1959), 7.

21. *House Documents*, 75 Cong., 2 sess., No. 385, p. 154. American Legion, California Department, *Proceedings of the Thirty-seventh Annual Convention*, San Diego, June, 1955, pp. 79-81. Zane B. Mathews, "What You Should Know about World Government," *The American Legion Magazine*, LVIII (May, 1955), 14-15, 50-53. *House Documents*, 84 Cong., 1 sess., No. 54, pp. 97-101. The San Francisco *Chronicle*, September 19, 1955, 11:1-2. *House Documents*, 83 Cong., 2 sess., No. 903, pp. 104-106.

22. *Supra*, pp. 22-28, 45-50. *The American Legion Magazine*, LXVI (June, 1959),

p. 4; J. Edgar Hoover, "We Must Choose Between Discipline and Barbarism," *The American Legion Magazine,* LXV (September, 1958), pp. 14-15, 48-50. The F.B.I. and the Legion have always maintained close relations. Lee Pennington upon retirement, headed the Legion's Washington, D.C. branch of the Counter-Subversive Activities Committee; *House Documents,* 79 Cong., 2 sess., No. 512, p. 33; *ibid.,* 84 Cong., 1 sess., No. 54, p. 143; Gray, *Inside the Legion,* pp. 210-211.

23. *Supra,* pp. 95-96. Rajani Palme Dutt, *Fascism and Social Revolution; A Study of the Economics and Politics of the Extreme Stages of Capitalism in Decay* (New York, 1935), p. 318; Daniel Lerner, Ithiel de Sola Pool, and George K. Schueller, *The Nazi Elite* (Stanford, California, 1951), p. 121; William Ebenstein, *Today's Isms*: *Communism, Fascism, Socialism* (New York, 1959), pp. 55-84; Alan Louis Charles Bullock, *Hitler; A Study in Tyranny,* p. 776. Erich Fromm, *Escape From Freedom,* pp. 161-164, 268, 274.

24. Richard Christie and Marie Jahoda, eds., "Studies in the Scope and Method of 'The Authoritarian Personality,'" *Continuities in Social Research* (Glencoe, Illinois, 1954), pp. 26, 121, 126, 193-195. People who scored high on the test were labeled fascist. Those who scored low automatically became democrats. It failed to measure the types of authoritarianism known to exist such as Communism or royalism. The question was raised if a real Nazi would have necessarily scored high on the scale. W. Edgar Gregory, "Authoritarianism and Authority," *The Journal of Abnormal and Social Psychology,* LI (1955), 641-643.

25. *Supra,* pp. 94-95. Gray, *Inside the Legion,* pp. 161-164. Gray quoted a telegram from the Ohio Department in support of Bradley. He also was sent into the streets of Indianapolis to sound out veterans' sentiment. It was almost all anti-Legion. Press reaction was against Stelle; *The New York Times,* February 2, 1946, 1:5, 14:2. Bradley said Stelle was irritated because the Veterans Administration would not put a hospital in Illinois where Stelle wanted it; *The Los Angeles Times,* Feb. 2, 1946, 4:12, and *ibid.,* Feb. 4, 1946, 1:1-2; *Time,* (Chicago), Feb. 11, 1946, pp. 21-22; *Newsweek,* Feb. 11, 1946, p. 55; *The Nation,* Feb. 9, 1946, p. 155.

26. American Legion, Special Committee on the Covenant of Human Rights and the United Nations, *The United Nations Educational Scientific and Cultural Organization; A Report to the National Executive Committee of the American Legion* (Indianapolis, 1955), pp. 1-45. Also Gordon D. Hall, *The Hate Campaign Against the U.N.: One World under Attack* (Boston, 1952), pp. 5-10; Carlson, *The Plotters,* pp. 149-150. *House Documents,* 84 Cong., 2 sess., No. 284, pp. 55-56. The Special Committee members reported that they were vilified by some top Legionnaires and hate groups. The San Francisco *Chronicle,* September 13, 1955, 22:1. *Life* covered the convention and editorially stated that the decision represented a "handful of kingmakers"; *Life Magazine* (Chicago), October 24, 1955, p. 44. In 1956, the Legion's national convention passed a resolution condemning *Life; House Documents,* 85 Cong., 1 sess., No. 43, p. 50. A Legion publication's editorial explained that Alger Hiss had helped to promote UNESCO; *The Firing Line* (Indianapolis), March 15, 1956, p. 22.

27. *Supra,* p. 22. H. H. Gerth and C. Wright Mills, eds., Max Weber, *From Max Weber*: *Essays in Sociology* (New York, 1946), pp. 245-252, 295-296.

28. *House Documents,* 77 Cong., 1 sess., No. 406, pp. 173-183. *Ibid.,* 80 Cong., 1 sess., No. 425, pp. 169-170; *ibid.,* 82 Cong., 2 sess., No. 313, p. 144; V.F.W., Americanism Department, *Subversive Organizations and Publications in the United States* (Kansas City, Missouri, 1959), pp 1-20. Gray, *Inside the Legion,* pp. 213-214. The Legion charges that Gray joined it with the deliberate idea of obtaining material to use against it later. *House Documents,* 83 Cong., 2 sess., No. 284, p. 52. *The American*

Legion Magazine, LV (August, 1953), 6-7. Victor Lasky, "How to Understand Communism," *The American Legion Magazine,* LV (August, 1953), 22-23, 55-57.

29. *House Documents,* 80 Cong., 2 sess., No. 775, pp. 159-161; *ibid.,* 81 Cong., 2 sess., No. 447, p. 122. One of the school's early counter-subversive experts was New Jersey Republican Congressman, J. Parnell Thomas. He was later imprisoned for accepting kickbacks from his Congressional office staff; *Newsweek Magazine,* December 19, 1949, p. 19. Gray, *Inside the Legion,* p. 228. Harvey Matusow, "Reds in Khaki," *The American Legion Magazine,* LIII (October, 1952), 14, 56-59. The San Francisco *Chronicle,* January 29, 1955, 1:7; *ibid.,* February 1, 1955, 1:4; *ibid.,* March 17, 1955, 1:7; the San Francisco *News,* February 4, 1955, 11:5.

30. Gellermann, *The Legion as Educator,* pp. 249-253, 264-266; Gray, *Inside the Legion,* pp. 239-255; Charles Kinsolving, "All Veterans Are Not Parasites," *The Forum,* XCII (November, 1934), 296-299.

31. Samuel Andrew Stouffer, *Communism, Conformity and Civil Liberties; A Cross-Section of the Nation Speaks* (New York, 1955), pp. 13-14, 23-25, 57, 87.

32. *Ibid.,* pp. 87, 91, 94-95, 217-219, 220-225.

33. Stouffer, *Communism, Conformity and Civil Liberties,* pp. 234-235.

34. *Ibid.* Also Robert Horn, "The Protection of Internal Security," *Public Administration Review; The Journal of the American Society for Public Administration,* XVI, No. 1 (Winter, 1956), 40-52. Horn's major criticism of Stouffer's analysis was his recommendation that education in the meaning of the Bill of Rights might solve public ignorance. Horn said that this was only a partial solution.

35. *Supra.,* p. 98. Also *House Documents,* 85 Cong., 2 sess., No. 303, p. 175. The Americanism Commission noted that Congress refused to investigate or condemn UNESCO. Both the V.F.W. and the M.O.W.W. followed suit; *ibid.,* 85 Cong., 2 sess., No. 305, pp. 199-203; M.O.W.W., *National Bulletin,* XXXIV (January, 1959), 6.

36. Fromm, *Escape From Freedom,* pp. 170-173.

<h2 style="text-align:center">Chapter VIII</h2>

1. *House Documents,* 77 Cong., 2 sess., No. 896, pp. 74-75; *ibid.,* 78 Cong., 1 sess., No. 364, pp. 7-8, 22, 118-119. The Legion did not start active recruitment of World War II veterans until 1944. *Ibid.,* 79 Cong., 1 sess., No. 43, pp. 181-187; *ibid.,* 80 Cong., 1 sess., No. 34, p. 32 By 1946, top Legionnaires still were uncertain about the younger veterans. Harry Moses, United States Steel executive and World War I veteran, told newsmen at the 1946 San Francisco convention, "After all this is a billion-dollar business. You don't just throw something that big over to a bunch of boys." The San Francisco *Chronicle,* October 6, 1946, "This Week Section," 2:3-4. *House Documents,* 79 Cong., 2 sess., No. 540, p. 136. The Legion was slower to advocate terminal leave pay for enlisted personnel; *ibid.,* 80 Cong., 1 sess., No. 34, p. 503.

2. American Veterans of World War II and Korea *AMVETS in Action* Washington, D.C., 1959), p. 2; Sam Stavisky, "The Veterans Make Their Choice," *Harper's Magazine,* CXCIII (1946), 251-258; Carlson, *The Plotters,* p. 313; Walter Davenport, "Twelve Million in Search of a Leader," *Colliers,* November 11, 1944, pp. 11, 64-67; Charles Guy Bolté, *The New Veteran* (New York, 1945), pp. 55-61, 71-73, 74-91; Gray, *Inside Story of the Legion,* pp. 15-27.

3. Davenport, *loc. cit.,* p. 11; Bolté, *The New Veteran,* pp. 46-53, 92-106.

4. Bolté, *The New Veteran,* pp. 46-53; Michael Straight, "Needed: World Government," *The A.V.C. Bulletin,* April 15, 1946, p. 4.

5. Bolte, *The New Veteran*, pp. 46-53, 96-107. 6. *Ibid.*

7. Davenport, *loc. cit.*, pp. 64-67; Stavisky, *loc cit.*, pp. 251-258; Victor Lasky, "The Veterans Organize," *The American Mercury*, LXIII (August, 1946), 167-173; *Time Magazine*, December 3, 1945, p. 23.

8. *The A.V.C. Bulletin* (New York), December 1, 1946, p. 6; Stavisky, *loc. cit.*, pp. 251-258; Carlson, *The Plotters*, p. 310. *The A.V.C. Bulletin*, March 1, 1946, p. 3; *ibid.*, May 15, 1946, p. 1; *ibid.*, July 1, 1946, p. 11. *Christian Century* (Chicago), July 3, 1946, pp. 830-831; *The Nation*, June 22, 1946, pp. 740-741; *The New Republic*, November 27, 1944 p. 695; *ibid.* October 7 1946 pp. 430-431.

9. *The A.V.C. Bulletin* March 15, 1946, p. 8; *ibid.*, July 1, 1946, p. 2. *House Documents*, 78 Cong., 1 sess., No. 364, p 355; *ibid*, 79 Cong., 1 sess., No. 182, pp. 102, 110-115; *The A.V.C. Bulletin*, July 15, 1946, pp. 1, 3; *The New Republic*, October 7, 1946, pp. 430-431; *The Nation*, March 1, 1947, p. 235; *The A.V.C. Bulletin*, March 1, 1947, pp. 1, 4; *ibid.*, October 1, 1946, p. 1; F. R. Hood to author, October 27, 1959, letter from Director of Information, Veterans Administration; Veterans Administration, "List of Recognized Organizations, Associations, and Other Agencies," *Bulletin 23-1*, March 27, 1959, p. 1.

10. *The Daily Worker* (New York), November 30, 1945, 11:1-5. Walter Bernstein, "Attacking Mr. Bolté," *The Nation*, January 19, 1946, pp. 65-67.

11. *Ibid.* Also E. A. Blackmore to author, November 4, 1959, letter from the National Adjutant of the American Legion; enclosure of sixteen photostats from the Legion's Americanism files that purported to show Communist domination of the N.C.U.L.L. Bolte, *The New Veteran*, pp. 75-77; Gray, *Inside the Legion*, pp. 71-93, 131-160, 179-190, 240; Merle Miller, "Rebutting Mr. Bernstein," *The Nation*, January 19, 1946, pp. 67-68.

12. *The Daily Worker*, November 30, 1945, 11:1-5; *The A.V.C. Bulletin*, November 15, 1946, p. 3; *ibid.*, December 1, 1946; *Time Magazine*, January 27, 1947, p. 20; *The New Republic*, June 30, 1947, p. 7; Daniel James, "The Battle of the A.V.C.," *The Nation*, June 14, 1947, pp. 706-708; *The A.V.C. Bulletin*, III (June, 1948), 4.

13. Julian H. Franklin, "Why I Broke with the Communists," *Harper's Magazine*, CXCIV (1947), 412-418; Charles G. Bolte, "We're On Our Own," *The Atlantic Monthly*, CLXXIX (1947), 27-33.

14. *The A.V.C. Bulletin*, III (September, 1948), 1, 5, 6; *ibid.*, III (November, 1948), 1, 2; *ibid.*, III (December, 1948), 5-7. American Veterans Committee, *Application Cards: Eligibility Requirements*, p. 2.

15. *The A.V.C. Bulletin*, IV (December, 1949), 5. "Controversial Little Cuss: The A.V.C.'s Bill Mauldin," *The New Yorker Magazine*, December 26, 1953, pp. 15-16. American Veterans Committee, *Handbook: Questions and Answers* (Washington, D.C., 1949), p. 1. *The A.V.C. Bulletin*, XIV (June, 1959), 1-4.

16. The A.V.C.'s position did not include surrender of American sovereignty to the U.N. In 1958, the group passed a resolution stating that such surrender would be impractical. As the strongest nation of the free world, the United States could not entrust the U.N. to define and execute American foreign policy. If it did so, it would abdicate its world responsibility; *The A.V.C. Bulletin*, XIII (April, 1958), 4.

17. R. Hal Silvers to author, October 26, 1959, letter from the American Veterans Committee National Secretary.

18. *The A.V.C. Bulletin*, II (September, 1947), 12; *ibid.*, II (October, 1947), 2; *ibid.*, III (March, 1948), 3. The American Veterans Committee, "Headlines and Stories of A.V.C. History," *The A.V.C. Bulletin*, XIII (June, 1958), 3. Not all

members agreed with the N.P.C.'s stand. Weyland M. Minot from Belmont, Massachusetts, "thanked God for McCarthy's guts," and wrote that those who had seen combat would support the Wisconsin senator; *ibid, VIII* (August-September, Joint issue, 1953), 2.

19. National Chairman Mickey Levine, "Report on Negro Veterans in the South," *American Veterans Committee* (Washington, D.C., 1956), pp. 1-10. *The A.V.C. Bulletin, XIII* (February, 1958), 1; *ibid., XIII* (January, 1958), 1. An examination of *The American Legion Magazine* issues from September, 1957 until December, 1958 failed to reveal any mention of the Faubus award by the National Headquarters' publication.

20. *The A.V.C. Bulletin, XIV* (September, 1959), 1, 2. The Forty and Eight Society, an all white inner group of Legionnaires, sponsors community service projects and is a fun-making group. A San Jose, California chapter recruited a Chinese-American Legionnaire. The national society suspended the chapter's charter. The Californians appealed to the Legion's National Executive Committee. The 1959 convention resolved that the N.E.C. force the Forty and Eight to eliminate its racially restrictive clause. The elite unit refused and the Legion's headquarters disenfranchised the fun-makers. They may no longer use the Legion's name and emblem in their activities. The N.E.C. was forced to deal with a national problem it preferred to ignore. A policy change occurred as a result. Yet, removal of restriction does not guarantee the end of explicit racial segregation. Under Legion policy posts choose their own members. White posts might remain just as they are. The national edict might signify more noise than action; The Palo Alto *Times* (Palo Alto, California), December 5, 1959, 1:2-3; *The American Legion Magazine, LXVII* (December, 1959), 28, 30.

21. Three editorials from the *Bulletin* illustrated the A.V.C.'s limited appeal. All three articles expressed pride in the committee's small size, its uniqueness and its function as a reception center for the liberal movement; Executive Director Kenneth Birkhead, "Taking Stock of AVC," *The A.V.C. Bulletin, XIII* (April, 1958), 2; Mickey Levine and Louis Warshaw, "AVC—Past—Present—Future," *The A.V.C. Bulletin, XIV* (June, 1959), 2.

22. Quoted in *The A.V.C. Bulletin, IX* (June, 1954), 3. The survey was conducted by the Teachers College Center for the Improvement of Group Procedures at Columbia University.

23. *Supra,* pp. 99-101. R. Hal Silvers to author, October 26, 1959, letter from the National Secretary of the A.V.C.; *The A.V.C. Bulletin, XIII* (March, 1958), 1; *ibid.,* XIII (October, 1958), 1; *ibid.,* XIII (November, 1958), 1, 3; *ibid.,* XIV (April, 1959), 1.

24. American Veterans of World War II, *Constitution and By-Laws* (Washington, D.C., 1944), p. 1; Stavisky, *loc. cit.,* pp. 251-258; Davenport, *loc. cit.,* pp. 11, 64-67; Lasny, *loc. cit.,* pp. 167-173; *Time Magazine,* December 3, 1945, p. 23; Carlson, *The Plotters,* pp. 310-313.

25. *The National AMVET* (Washington, D.C.), I (June, 1946), 12-13; Stavisky, *loc. cit.,* p. 253-258; Davenport, *loc. cit.,* p. 11; Carlson, *The Plotters,* pp. 313-315; *Time Magazine,* December 3, 1945, p. 23; *The National AMVET,* I (June, 1946), 19, 21, 23, 24.

26. *The National AMVET, IV* (February, 1950), 2, 7; *ibid.,* IV (December, 1950), 1, 4. The international veterans' league was pledged to seek peace and was anti-

Communist. There were no racial bars to membership. It sought international co-operation of all types; *The A.V.C. Bulletin*, XIII May, 1958), 3; *ibid.*, XIV (June, 1959), 3; *ibid.*, XIV (January, 1959), 1. *The National AMVET*, I (June 1946), 19 21, 23, 24. The American Veterans of World War II and Korea, *AMVETS in Action* (Washington, D.C., 1959), pp. 46-48.

27. *The National AMVET*, II (April, 1947), 7; *ibid.*, III (March, 1948), 6.

28. *The A.V.C. Bulletin*, IV August-September, Joint issue, 1949), 1, 2-3; *ibid.*, IV (October, 1949), 1, 4. Harold Russell and Victor Rosey, *Victory in My Hands* (New York, 1949), pp. 256-280; *The National AMVET*, IV (February, 1950), 2, 7; *ibid.*, IV (December, 1950), 1, 4; *ibid.*, V (January, 1951), 4.

29. *The National AMVET*, V (January, 1951), 4; *ibid.*, V (October, 1951), 2.

30. *Collier's Magazine* (Springfield, Ohio), September 17, 1954, p. 98. Amvets claimed, in 1950, that they had 200,000 members: *The National AMVET*, IV (October, 1950), 2.

31. American Veterans of World War II and Korea, *Constitution and By-Laws, as Amended August 24, 1958* (Washington, D.C., 1958), pp. 1-8. Warner and Lunt, *Social Life of a Modern Community*, I, 116-121.

32. *Congressional Record*, CIII, 7913-7914, May 28, 1957; American Veterans of World War II and Korea, *Your Legacy—U.S.A.* (Washington, D.C., 1957), pp. iii, 1-2.

33. AMVETS, *Your Legacy*, pp. 1-2; American Veterans of World War II and Korea, *Group Leaders Information* (Washington, D.C., 1957), p. 1. American Veterans of World War II and Korea, Americanism Program, *Americanism Materials Available from National Headquarters* (Washington, D.C., 1959), pp. 1-5.

34. AMVETS, *Your Legacy*, pp. 1, 3-5, 9, 10-11, 22-23.

35. AMVETS, *Americanism Program Newsletter*, April, 1957, pp. 1-8.

36. *Ibid.*, p. 4.   37. *Supra*, p. 109.

38. Veterans' societies sometimes might be evasive about membership. Both Amvets and the A.V.C. have not recently published definite figures. The A.V.C. usually states that its small membership is a virtue. The Legion and the V.F.W have had their troubles, too. In 1957, the Legion's National Headquarters ordered 3,520,000 membership cards. Of these, 2,558,172 were used; *House Documents*, 85 Cong., 2 sess., No. 303, pp. 116-123. The V.F.W.'s membership committee announced in 1957 that post incorporation was on a downward trend. Twenty per cent of the membership dropped out yearly. Between 1952 and 1957, an estimated one million men left the V.F.W.; *House Documents*, 85 Cong., 2 sess., No. 305, p. 110, 123-128, 373. In 1956, against the opposition of the old-line veterans' organizations, the Amvets opposed a pension bill; United States Congress, *House Committee on Veterans Affairs, Bills Relating to Non-Service-Connected Pensions for Veterans and Their Dependents (All Wars)*, 84 Cong., 2 sess., Hearings, February 27, 28, 29 and March 1, 1956 pp. 2649-2686, 2687-2696, 2709-2710, 2779-2785, 2786-2796, 2797-2798.

CHAPTER IX

1. Grodzins, *The Loyal and the Disloyal*, pp. 5-6, 24, 29-30, 47.

2. *Ibid.*, pp. 68-69.

3. *House Documents*, 85 Cong., 2 sess., No. 367, pp. 71-78.

4. The decline of the older veterans' influence might be due to the fact that the need for group security was passing in America. Perhaps the mobile society was subsiding into some form of order; see Rowland Berthoff, "The American Social Order:

A Conservative Hypothesis," *The American Historical Review*, LXV (1960), 495-514. Only about seventeen or eighteen per cent of America's twenty-two million veterans were in organizations; Hansen, *1960 World Almanac*, p. 745. Despite the fact that the veterans' societies were urban in origin, their main strength in 1959 appeared to lie in rural areas. The Legion's 1957 membership figures, when checked against the 1950 census, showed that approximately three and a half per cent of an agrarian state's population belonged. By contrast, under two per cent of an urban state's citizens joined. Such figures were not conclusive, but they might indicate a correlation between rural conservatism and Legion policy. This subject needs additional study; *House Documents*, 85 Cong., 2 sess., No. 303, p. 424.

5. *The National AMVET*, I (September, 1946), 6; ibid., II, (March, 1947), 5; *ibid.*, V (October, 1951), 2.

6. M.O.W.W. *National Bulletin*, XXXIV (September, 1958), 8.

7. David M. Potter, *People of Plenty* (Chicago, 1954), pp. 84, 99, 105, 106-107, 109, 116, 119-120, 134. Potter stated that the United States possessed an abundance of material wealth which afforded great opportunities for enrichment. Americans developed a compulsion to utilize their wealth. In their drive for material goods, power and security, Americans often were never satisfied with their station in life. The resultant insecurity had a corrosive effect on American life. A different interpretation arrived at much the same conclusion; Mead, *And Keep Your Powder Dry*, pp. 27-53.

INDEX

A

Addams, Jane, 47f, 123
Adorno, T. W., 95-97
Adventure Magazine, 32f, 40, 125
Alger, Russell, 17
Aliens. *See* Immigration
All-American Conference to Combat Communism, 98
America First, 67
American Civil Liberties Union (A.C.L.U.), 47f, 50, 58, 64, 131
American Expeditionary Force (A.E.F.), 36, 38ff
American Legion, 38-41, 100, 77-79, 126, 133, 136; before 1915, 29, 32-36, 127; and disabled veterans, 50-52; its Americanism, 55-67 *passim*, 71-85 *passim*, 114-15; Americanism Commission, 57ff, 64-65, 70-71, 74-88 *passim*, 98f, 117; 135; its magazine, 57f, 70, 75f, 84, 86, 88, 96, 99, 130f; National Executive Committee (N.E.C.), 77-79, 98, 100, 144; and immigration, 85-89, 130-31, 137; and counter subversion, 92-94, 99, 105; and authoritarianism, 94, 96-99; and veterans of World War II and Korea, 103-11 *passim*, 142, 145f; mentioned, 2, 43f, 46, 72, 129
American Medical Association, 66
American Officers of the Great War, 45
American Veterans Committee (A.V.C.), 104-6, 108f, 143ff; its *Bulletin*, 104-109 *passim;* National Planning Committee, 106f, 109, 144; its Americanism, 107-8, 111, 116; mentioned, 2, 132, 135f
American Veterans of Foreign Service, 26-27
American Veterans of World War II and Korea (Amvets), 2, 108-11, 116, 135, 145
Americanism Commission. *See under* American Legion
Americans for Democratic Action, 99
Amvets, 2, 108-11, 116

B

Baldridge, C. LeRoy, 64-66, 133
Bancroft, George, 6, 10, 119
Belknap, R. R., 93, 139
Bernstein, Walter, 105
Beveridge, Albert J., 11, 119
Blakely, George W., 93
Blayney, Lindsey, 60
Blount, Hamilton H., 21-22, 122
Bolivar, Simon, 5
Bollenbeck, Joseph W., 96
Bolte, Charles G., 104ff, 119, 132
Borah, William E., 48, 92
Boxer Rebellion, 22
Bradley, Omar, 97, 100, 141
Bryan, William Jennings, 18, 121
Bryant, William Cullen, 5
Buchenwald, 10
Buckley, William, 99
Bunche, Ralph, 107
Bullock, C. Seymour, 125-6
Burgess, John W., 11, 119
Burnham, James, 99
Butler, Smedley, 93

C

Calhoun, John C., 7-8
Chadwick, Stephen F., 65-66
Chafee, Zechariah, Jr., 48
Chaillaux, Homer, 64-66, 91f, 94, 105, 132
Chambers, Whittaker, 99
Charlton, Charles M., 114
China, 87, 90
Civil War, 4, 8-9, 14, 19, 45, 56, 85
Clark, Bennett Champ, 39ff
Clark, Bennett Champ, Jr., 39, 127
Clinnin, John V., 62
Cold War, 14, 42, 54, 96, 101, 118
Cole, Frederick W., 21
Collins, Seaborn, 96
Colorado Society of the Army of the Philippines, 27
Columbia Teacher's College, 84

147